About the Author

Paul Mooney began his working life as a butcher in Dublin. He then moved into production management, working for several years with a British multinational company. He subsequently joined General Electric and worked in a number of Human Resource positions.

After GE, he worked with Sterling Drug as Personnel Manager in their highly successful Irish plant. Subsequently, as Human Resource Director for the Pacific Rim, he had responsibility for South-East Asia.

In 1991, Paul established PMA Consulting, specialising in customised organisation and management development programmes. His client list reads like a "who's who" of Irish and multinational corporations with assignments in more than 20 countries. Paul is the author of two previous books — *Amie: The True Story of Adoption in Asia* (1990) and *Developing the High Performance Organisation* (1996) — and he has written numerous booklets and business articles.

Paul holds the National Diploma in Industrial Relations from the National College of Ireland, a Postgraduate Diploma and a PhD from Trinity College, Dublin. In 1997 he was made a Fellow of the Institute of Personnel and Development.

THE EFFECTIVE CONSULTANT

How to Develop the High Performance Organisation

Paul Mooney

Oak Tree Press
Dublin

Oak Tree Press
Merrion Building
Lower Merrion Street
Dublin 2, Ireland
www.oaktreepress.com

© 1999 Paul Mooney

A catalogue record of this book is
available from the British Library.

ISBN 1 86076 121 6

Printed in Britain by MPG Books, Bodmin, Cornwall

Contents

Preface

The Birth of an Idea

This book was "conceived" in the Clarence Hotel, Dublin, over breakfast in June 1997. I had been speaking with a client about a recently installed recognition programme. From concept to installation, the programme was well thought-through and brilliantly executed by a local manager working in an "internal consultancy" role. I asked the client if he would allow us to "write it up" as a case study of local initiative — to be used in a Management Development Programme that we were designing. While he did not know it at the time, he'd sown the seed for a more ambitious project.

Later, in 1998, I was asked to teach a couple of classes in Dublin City University on "Effective Consulting". After initially agreeing to do the sessions, the panic set in — *what will I talk about?* From these two initial experiences, the structure for this book slowly began to take shape.

Understanding What Works — and What Doesn't

The primary rationale for the book is to evaluate a range of actual organisation development consulting projects to see "what works" and "what doesn't work" in the real world. Using real cases provides a practical learning exercise on effective organisation change practices, from the perspective of both the consultant and the organisation. Through our work with a range of clients, my consultancy firm has come across literally dozens of outstanding organisation innovations. PMA Consulting have been directly involved in designing some of these initiatives; in others we were simply in the right place at the right time to see excellent practice in action. This book provides a vehicle to present the lessons learned to a wider audience. It should be of value to both external and internal consultants and to organisations wishing to improve their performance.

While I have peppered the text with specific examples, I have changed company names and certain details to protect confidentiality.

Learning from Error: Oops!

"You should try to learn from the mistakes of others; you couldn't possibly live long enough to make them all yourself." — Anon

We have also encountered many poor practices and mistakes in organisation change initiatives (some of which we were directly responsible for!). The discussion and publication of these may help other management teams or consultants avoid driving into similar culs-de-sac.[1]

Toward More Effective Consulting Relationships

If you are already engaged in internal/external consulting, the lessons presented should allow you to:

- Avoid no-win consulting situations — where your reputation can be damaged.

- Start off on the right foot — by managing the contracting phase really well.

- Ensure your recommendations are more frequently implemented — principally by developing client commitment to the solutions proposed.

- Make enough money to ensure your financial health in old age (there's only one thing worse than being old — it's being old *and* poor!).

If you are a manager in an organisation, this book should help you to:

- Avoid spending money on consulting assignments that don't add value.

---

[1] During the writing of this book, one consultant asked, "Why would you write a book 'showing your hand'? The methods detailed are part of your intellectual property." We understand and respect this point of view. However, a key part of our business philosophy is continuous improvement. Writing and reflecting on our experiences allows us to make sense of our own consulting methods. We have no problem in sharing this with our partners in the business community.

- Ensure change projects have maximum performance impact.

- Get the most value from external consultants by
  developing a partnership which is beneficial to both
  parties.

Thanks and Absolution

When over eight years of consulting experience gets
"rolled up", it is not always clear just who and where
you've stolen the individual ideas from.

Thanks are due to the following consultants:
Tony Brady, Sean Brophy, Paul Dooley, Paul
Donovan, Paddy Feeney, Bob Fulmer, Rick Gilkey,
Conor Hannaway, Gerry Lyons, Eddie Molloy,
Ed Naughton, Sean Ruth and Frank Scott-Lennon.

On the client side: Joe Banks, David Brown,
Cathy Buffini, Pat Casey, Tom Comerford, Des
Crowley, Pat Cunneen, Tom Doyle, June Duffy, Kyle
Greer, John Guinan, Joe Harford, Richard Hoare,
Donnacha Hurley, Dave Keenan, Larry Kelly, Pat
Lunny, John McCloskey, Sandra McDevitt, Peter
Mulholland, Tony Murray, Liam Nolan, Mary
O'Connor, Clare O'Hagan, Tony O'Shea, John
Philips, Mon Segismundo, Joe Walsh and Catherine
Whelan have all added to the richness of the ideas
and experiences presented.

To all of the above we offer the standard absolu-
tion from responsibility for errors.

This Book is Dedicated to . . .

Much of the material in this book has been learned directly from clients. My thanks to the individual managers who sweated the details, pushed, cajoled and installed the organisation development initiatives detailed. You can't keep a good manager down. As I write this book, they are out there — beavering, tinkering, continually improving, looking for better ways to manage their people and their organisations.

Introduction

What Are You Buying?
The Role of the Management Consultant

"I've looked at life from both sides now, from win and lose and still somehow, it's life's illusions I recall, I really don't know life at all"
— Joni Mitchell, *Both Sides Now*, 1967

What is a Consultant?

We start with the (somewhat boring) definitional piece around the appropriate consulting role. Firstly, there is no universally accepted definition of management consulting. Almost every knowledgeable person at one time or another serves as a "consultant" to someone who is struggling with a problem that is confusing or distressing. Just as there are many different types of people and approaches in the medical field, the consulting world is populated by an array of approaches, techniques and personalities.

Most Staff People Operate as Consultants

In organisations, most people in staff roles are really consultants, even if they don't officially use this title. Staff people function in most organisations by recommending, assisting or advising line managers *over whom they have no direct control.*

Consulting v Managing: Is There a Difference?

A consultant is sometimes defined as a person who is trying to influence an individual, group or organisation, but who has no direct power to make changes or implement programmes. In contrast, a manager is someone who has direct control over the "action". Thus, one view of the consulting role is as follows:

> The moment you take direct control over a project or programme, you cease to operate as a consultant and you are acting as a manager. The key to understanding the consultant role is to see the difference between a consultant and a manager.[1]

Management Consulting is Not Easy to Define

Does the above provide a good definition of consulting? Is it a simple split between the power to recommend and the power to do? I don't think so. While this may be a good definition of process con-

---

[1] *Source:* this is the central thesis of a number of books explaining the difference between management consulting and management. See, for example, Cockman, Evans and Reynolds (1992), *Client-Centred Consulting*, McGraw-Hill.

sulting, it is not an accurate definition of the actual role that many consultants play in organisations — some of whom exercise quite an amount of direct power.

While some definitions are put forward as being definitive (a management consultant *should do X or Y*), in practice it is difficult to be absolute; there is a huge range of consulting behaviour across the spectrum from *hands-on/directive* to more *consultative* or *process type* behaviour. To understand the role of consultants, it is helpful to differentiate between a "politically correct" view that consultants *must* empower their clients (e.g. not take control of situations) alongside the contradictory view that "anything which the clients feel adds value is legitimate" (including consultants taking complete control of the situation). What emerges is that the role of management consultants can encompass a number of different types of advice — some of which are quite different and even contradictory.

Probably the best way to illustrate "process consulting" is to demonstrate its application. The following vignette is told in the book *Tales for Trainers* by Margaret Parkin.[2]

What is Process Consulting?

In the days when terms like Organisation Development and Process Consultancy were relatively new, one of the great gurus was Chris Argyris. A smallish British firm decided that it needed some

---

2 1998, London: Kogan Page.

Organisational Development, whatever that was, and saved up its pennies to buy one whole day of Argyris's time.

The entire board assembled to hear him speak. Argyris took his seat and was silent. After a while one of the board members stood up and began to describe their problems. Argyris remained silent.

Another board member then began to speak. And another, and another . . . but still nothing from Argyris. Soon the flip chart had been covered with words and diagrams and everyone except Argyris was engaged in debate.

His silence continued over lunch. At three o'clock, the Managing Director had finished an elaborate diagram of a current problem and Argyris stood up, went to the flip chart, and picked up the magic marker left by the MD. A hushed silence fell on the group.

Argyris capped the magic marker and, as he replaced it in its trough, said: "You know, if you don't put the caps back on these things, they dry up." That was the last thing he said.

On one level, this is client empowerment *par excellence*. However, you can see the process consultant's dilemma of convincing a client that they have any product to offer (at least in the short term). Many companies see process consulting as a managerial form of "The Emperor's New Clothes".

How Can a Consultant be of Maximum Value to the Client?[3]

Another way to approach the question of the appropriate role is to ask: "How should a consultant function to be of maximum value to the client?" Because each client is different and each problem is different, consultants potentially have a wide range of functions. These can be illustrated as a *Continuum of Consultant Behaviours*. The concept here is that the client and consultant must find the correct mix of their combined experience that will illuminate the problem and allow them to follow through.

CONTINUUM OF CONSULTANT BEHAVIOURS

Client-centred interaction ⟵⟶ Consultant-centred interaction

Use of client's experience and knowledge

Use of consultant's specialised experience and knowledge

Refuses to become involved / Listens / Reflects / Clarifies / Interprets / Probes / Gathers / Diagnoses / Adds new data / Identifies options / Proposes criteria / Prescribes / Recommends / Plans implementation

---

[3] In the discussion we have drawn heavily on the work of Warren H. Schmidt and Arthur V. Johnston, *A Continuum of Consultancy Styles*. The original concepts have been somewhat modified.

Client-centred (Process) Consulting

Behaviour toward the *left* of the continuum can be thought of as client-centred and is sometimes referred to as "process consulting". Here the *client* has within him/her the basic experience necessary to understand, analyse and find the solution to the problem. The need is for someone to provide a setting and be a sounding board to support efforts to sort out the client's own experience. Outside of the business world, much psychotherapy/non-directive counselling is of this type.

Consultant-centred (Prescriptive) Consulting

Behaviour toward the *right* can be thought of as consultant-centred (often referred to as "prescriptive consulting"). Here it is the *consultant's* specialised knowledge that is most relevant. The farther the client moves to the right, the more the consultant functions in an "expert" role. Medical doctors, car mechanics and barristers are frequently expected to provide this kind of consultation.

Factors Affecting the Mix of Client–Consultant Experience

The factors that determine the appropriate position on the continuum for any given consultancy assignment fall into two categories.

- Factors unique to the client/situation

- Factors unique to the consultant.

Factors Unique to the Client/Situation

Behaviour toward the *right* of the continuum (consultant-centred) is appropriate where the client has little experience or understanding of the problem (and recognises this), where the client has a speedy need for help (an additional "pair of hands") or where the client is experienced in using consultants (avoids becoming overly dependent).

However, behaviour toward the *right* tends to be less effective in a situation where the client has a high need for independence, a need to understand and learn about the problem, a need for ownership of the solution and where the client's decision-taking norms are violated by being "given" a solution. Behaviour toward the right will also tend to be less effective where the penalty for an incorrect solution is high, the system affected by the problem is complex and where the problem has a long-term perspective (i.e. is not simple to resolve).

Factors Unique to the Consultant

Behaviour toward the right of the continuum (consultant-centred) is often used in a situation where the consultant has depth of experience, a well-established position in his/her profession and a high need to own the solution (often where the consultant's natural style tends towards being prescriptive). This type of consulting can also be useful where there is a high degree of certainty about the "problem" and about the likely outcome/preferred solution. For example, an internal manager may be using a consultant to push a change agenda which the manager has already identified. Working in this way assumes that the consultant's understanding of the client's organisation, technology, structure, norms and values is high.

However, behaviour toward the right will be less effective where the consultant's values are based around helping a client grow and develop (preventing dependency by promoting self-sufficiency). Another obvious potential danger is that the consultant treats the client like a "patient" or that this "single view of the universe" comes to dominate the contract.

The Consultant's Intervention Style Needs to be Custom-built for the Client/Situation

The Schmidt and Johnston model is useful in helping us to understand that a range of factors influence the "correct choice" of intervention style. It also allows managers to determine what will work best in relation to their specific problem. In management consulting, there is no organisational equivalent of "one size fits all".

What is the "Correct" Consulting Model? A Search for the Holy Grail

There are few absolutes in this area — just a number of tensions that need to be continually managed. We should recognise that some consulting methods are driven by underlying/unspoken values. Some of the common dilemmas are sketched below:

- The heavy diagnostic models favoured by many major consulting companies (with armies of consultants spending vast amounts of "diagnostic" time on the client site) are sometimes driven by economic considerations (e.g. junior consultants can be billed at high hourly rates).[4]

- The process consulting model (where a consultant empowers the client and does not take an active interventionist role) is often put forward as the best (or even the only) way to help organisations learn and change. Proponents of this view (such as Professor Ed Schein at the Harvard Business School or Dr Eric Miller at the Tavistock Institute in London) have an explicit political belief that organisations should learn to help themselves; the underlying belief is that the only legitimate role of a consultant is to help clients fix future problems from their own resources. Consultants who play an "expert" role are seen to disempower (and ultimately damage) their clients by creating dependency.

An analogy can be made here with a son or daughter coming home from school and struggling with their homework. A parent could say, "*OK, I'll do the maths for you*". Even if you got it 100 per cent correct — would this be the right thing to do? Most people would argue "no" — the child has been deprived of learning. Process con-

---

[4] For a terrific discussion on this see James O'Shea and Charles Madigan (1997), *Dangerous Company*, Nicholas Brealey Publishing Limited.

sultants argue that exactly the same rationale holds for the management consulting role; they are reluctant to "do the maths" for clients.[5]

- Some consultants believe that *anything* which a client requests and which they can (legally) provide is a legitimate service. They dispense with the moral argument essentially in the same way that publishing companies sell magazines. If *you* want it, *you* buy it. *We* are happy to sell it to you. This was summarised in the marketing advice which I heard from one consultant who suggested:

  The very best clients are those who have a strategic weakness, who recognise this and are prepared to pay for help to "shore it up". That's where the real money is.

- Some consulting services are invisible and selling "invisible" products is not easy. For example, in process consulting the product may be an understanding of group dynamics within a senior management team (including feelings, anxieties and unconscious processes which drive particular behaviours). Trying to package or even explain this is not easy. This invisibility factor may force consultants into a more directive/"visible added-value"

---

[5] By disempowering clients, "prescriptive consulting" is seen to treat managers like children. Many clients have described this feeling to me, where teams of consultants have been brought in to "sort them out".

role, partly for the sake of justifying their existence.[6]

That's why it is *always* easier to work with a confident internal client. Managers with less confidence normally continually worry about the cost/packaging/perception of the consultant and sometimes force consultants into a form of "grandstanding" to justify their existence.

- The expert (doctor/patient) model is seductive from the consultant's perspective, based as it is on the assumption that, de facto, the consultant is cleverer than the client. It is sometimes even an outward justification for the fees charged! In a hospital, watch the medical consultant doing the rounds with hordes of awestruck helpers in tow. It must be wonderful to dispense caustic wit and expertise to the medical minions and highly dependent patients alike. Some business consultants are also guilty of creating primitive dependency relationships, often by selling packaged "social science" solutions to a gullible business audience.[7]

---

[6] One of the reasons why consultants spend so much effort in "packaging" their products is because of the invisible nature of the service. Sometimes clients end up buying four-colour brochures rather than expert partnership help.

[7] The issue of "consulting flavours of the month" (e.g. re-engineering) is discussed in some detail later.

So, What's the Answer? What is the "Correct" Consulting Role?

In the final analysis, this is a philosophical debate. There is no single "right" way to help another person or a group solve a problem. Effective consulting is a partnership with a client in a quest for clarity or a course of action which is presently hidden. The specific help needed will vary from person to person and from situation to situation. To the question "what is the correct consulting model?", the answer is, "it depends". The best way to avoid any potential role conflict for the client and the consultant is to negotiate the respective roles in advance, making this an explicit part of the entry phase.[8]

The issue of role clarity often surfaces at some point in a consultancy relationship. Ignoring it won't make it disappear. If unresolved, it can damage the overall process and even the long-term relationship.

---

[8] This is "medicine" which consultants do not always like to swallow for two reasons. Firstly, the debate is somewhat philosophical and some clients have little appetite for this. It may even confirm a bias that consultants are theory merchants while the clients are trying to resolve "real" problems. Secondly, there is often a high degree of pressure to drive on with the consulting assignment. Sometimes consultants need to resist this front-end performance pressure (explored later in the text); sometimes they simply have to "cave in" and work out the role as they go.

Consulting "à la Carte": Allow the Client to Choose the Specific Role Support they Need

At the front-end of new assignments, consultants often talk with clients about a potential range of roles in order to select whichever is most appropriate. For example, in relation to organisation change projects, the most successful assignments my own consultancy have been involved in took a joint project team (client and consultant) approach. This normally ensures that the end "product" is high quality, meets client expectations and delivers real change. Organisation change projects are ultimately owned by the organisation for whom they are prepared; clients' direct participation and leadership of projects is essential to ensure front-end ownership and back-end follow-through (the Achilles' Heel of consulting assignments).

However, we have also been involved in a number of more prescriptive consulting assignments — which worked equally well (albeit on shorter, more defined projects). In assignments there are certain segments of work where consultants typically play the primary role; in other contracts, the management team take the lead. It follows that the consulting role can have one or a number of separate dimensions (see below).

1. Process Definition/Design

In conjunction with the local management team, consultants "firm up" on the project rationale/objectives and lay out a process that will deliver against this. This might involve the detailed design of individual segments, preparation of documentation to be used during the data-gathering phase, for training sessions, etc.

2. Process Facilitation

Consultants can facilitate the improvement process during the diagnostic (and later) phases to ensure that the key emerging points are understood, the outcome of meetings is recorded in a professional format, etc. The key consulting role here is to be authentic, clarifying progress, ensuring that all "roadblocks" are made discussible (a point we return to in some detail later).

3. Acting as a Coach/Sounding Board

This entails the consultant getting sufficiently involved in the substance of projects to challenge conclusions and essentially raise the thinking. This element of the consulting role can help to build management capability by imparting tools and techniques that can subsequently be used by the organisation's own managers.

4. Implementation

Some consulting companies manage the implementation phase. Clients may need/request what is referred to in construction as "turnkey" projects — i.e. all the work is done in advance, and this simply has to be handed over to the client.

Understanding Consulting Style

In assessing the best way to help a particular client, consultants might usefully ask themselves questions like:

- "Am I helping my client to see crucial problems more clearly and in a broader perspective?"

- "Am I really needed here — or am I doing the work which could be done more properly (and less expensively) by my client i.e. is my client depending on me too heavily?"

- "Do I have a consistent tendency to use one style of behaviour with many clients in many situations — and what does this tell me about myself?"

Organisational Impact

Similarly, managers can usefully address the following questions:

- "How good is this particular consultant?"[9]

- "Do particular 'types' of consultants seem to work well within this organisation?"

- "What *exactly* are we looking for?"

- "Can we set measurable performance goals for the consulting assignment — which will allow us to track progress?"

---

[9] I am constantly amazed that managers who would not dream of hiring an employee without full reference-checking often ignore this step in engaging consultants. The manager should speak with previous clients and explore both "competence" and "chemistry" issues.

Moving into the Arena: The Five-Phase Consulting Model

Now that the role theory is out of the way (phew!), let's move into the arena. Each consulting project, whether it lasts five minutes or five years, normally goes through five phases,[10] as illustrated in the figure on the next page. The remainder of this book details each of the steps in sequence.

---

[10] Unless of course, it is "cancelled" at some point. Although shown in sequential order, real life projects do not always follow such a neat pattern. For example, "Data Collection" is not something that happens at a particular moment (Phase 2) but continues throughout an assignment. Similarly, in large-scale projects there is often a need to put some "early wins" in place (a Phase 4 task), which, strictly speaking, is out of the sequence of the model proposed. However, the five-phase model shown represents the "logical" flow of a consulting assignment and is the structure followed throughout this book.

THE FIVE-PHASE CONSULTING MODEL

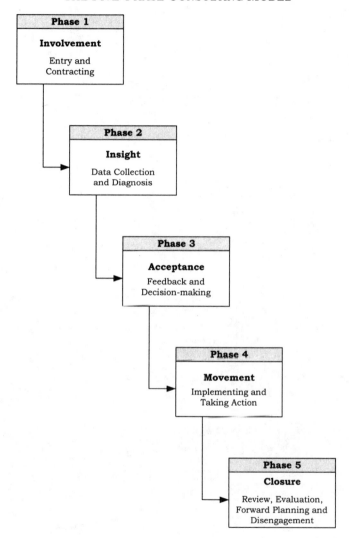

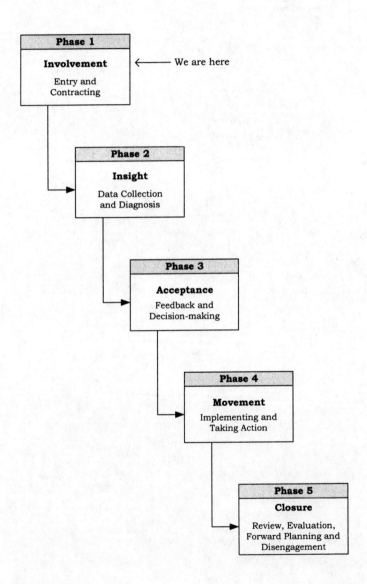

Phase 1

Involvement
Entry and Contracting

---

*"If at first you don't succeed,
you are running about average"*
— M.H. Anderson

The purpose of the entry and contracting phase

1. Create links between the consultant and potential clients.

2. Determine if there is a "chemistry fit" between consultant and client.

3. See if there are internal organisation issues that a consultant could support.

4. Negotiate/clarify the terms of reference for a successful consulting contract.

Before the consultant can develop any "high performance" consulting solutions, they must gain access to clients. The following points are a summary of the lessons my consultancy firm has learned over the past number of years.[1]

Know thine own product (i.e. *what* are you selling?)

On starting PMA Consulting in 1991, I began to "network" with all of the Irish personnel managers who I had met prior to living abroad. It seemed an easy "entry point", a good way to get to know what was happening in the marketplace and to generate some initial business. One lunch partner was John Guinan — now head of HR at Bank of Ireland. Midway through our meeting, John asked the question: "So, what are you selling?" I replied (somewhat indignantly): "I am not selling anything!" John's response was typically straightforward: "Then why are we here?" It was an early lesson in marketing.

Every consultant must decide:

1. What "product" they are selling *and*

2. How this will benefit the client.

Unless they have a defined product, it is difficult for the consultant to gain entry. Hardly revolutionary marketing thinking. However, some consultants are reluctant to talk about "products" and "selling" — almost as if this demeans the profession of management consulting. Once the consultant has gained

---

[1] Some of the points made in the following sections apply more directly to "external" consultants. However, as all managers are potential purchasers of consulting, the points made should be generally useful.

entry on a specific assignment, it may be possible to move into a more generalist consulting role (i.e. a less specific project) — but this is a tough sell at the early stages when the client does not really know the consultant or their potential. In the early days, one potential client accused me of "selling a bucket of smoke".

Selling a Recognised Product: Upsides and Downsides

Some consulting services are invisible. Over a chicken pasta dish, try to convince someone that you sell "depth understanding of issues" or "excellent problem resolution". Try to market "judgement" as a Unique Selling Proposition. You can almost see the mental shutters being pulled down as lunch partners decide that there is nothing on offer. You end up not getting the business *and* paying for the lunch.

The lesson: Most consultants sell a recognisable product. While this, in itself, is not a problem, it can become one when all organisation issues are diagnosed to dovetail with the "solution-for-sale". There are a number of consulting companies who specialise in particular areas (e.g. management competencies) and who diagnose all organisations' ills through this extremely narrow lens. It is very frustrating (and all too common) to find clients who have been "sold" a solution that does not fit the problem they need to address. Reminder: *When the only tool you have is a hammer, it's surprising how many of your problems look like nails.*

Companies usually wish to buy *something* which has worked elsewhere. What they should buy is *someone* who has worked elsewhere. In other words, the key benefit is the insight and the working method of the consultant — not the particular package. A consulting company that can demonstrate an up-to-date knowledge of the literature and success in working through complex, unique problems elsewhere is usually a better bet than buying the "Seven Pillars of Excellence" model, tweaked to fit your particular business. We can illustrate this point with a specific example.

Say Cheese: The Food Manufacturer Who Was Not Smiling

In the early 1990s I had a very seductive phone call from a large food manufacturer. This household brand name producer had attempted to install a Total Quality Management (TQM) process in a plant in rural Ireland. They had worked with a reputable consulting group who led a major change effort — over two years — to increase product yields and move towards a "zero defects" culture in all parts of the operation. After two years of working to install a "TQM" process, product quality had remained "about the same or possibly marginally disimproved". I received the call to "come and rescue the project".

I rode in on my white horse from Dublin — ready to slay all organisation dragons. Specifically, I wanted to detect the flaws in the content or the implementation process *pursued by the other consulting group. After a reasonably detailed review, I concluded that both were flawless — with one caveat. They would work fine in a company that* wanted to *install a TQM process; within the client company, there was almost no appetite for this.*

The background was as follows. The company had been experiencing a number of manufacturing quality problems and wanted to address these. They contacted a consulting company who specialised in installing TQM systems. Voilà! Their diagnosis showed that the company needed a full-blown, belt-and-braces TQM system, and that is exactly what they got. In reality, that is exactly what they did not *need. The proof of the pudding was that it did not work as it had so little internal management support (a fundamental requirement to the successful installation of TQM and most other organisation change programmes).*

We continually come across companies who have been sold a pup when they wanted a kitten. It does not work. The solution has to custom fit the specific problem and the environment or the "body will reject it".

Pre-packaged Solutions "Sold" by Consulting Companies

Consultants often sell "solutions" as a packaged product — shrink-wrapped, off-the-shelf. While some customisation may take place, this is often at the margins; e.g. incorporating a company's logo into participants' materials on a cover page of a training programme. The baseline materials themselves are often repackaged for several clients with little investigation of the core issues. After initial selling in, the particular "solution" (Teambuilding, Business Process Redesign, 360° feedback, etc.) is then internally marketed within the client company. In the worst case scenario, a company ends up with "solutions looking for problems".

Part of the problem is organisation expectations of an instant solution, and this is often oversold during the entry and contracting phase. Where a premium is put on effective time usage, getting to the heart of the matter quickly is seen as a key skill.

In a society where fast food is a growth industry, speed is a competitive weapon. There is an aversion to time-wasting and even to certain words that convey the impression of slowness; e.g. "analysis" (read as "paralysis"), "academic" ("professional" or "out of touch") or "diagnosis" ("wheel spinning"). Of course speed is important — but if it is the only selection criterion for the use of consultants, you simply get to the wrong decision more quickly!

A subsidiary issue here is confusion of means with ends. A good example of this is the plethora of "teambuilding" packages now on sale. This has almost become the organisational equivalent of snake-oil, a cure-all for every ailment. Teambuilding, a means to high output and performance, has become an end in itself — as if the purpose of business was to create happier groups of staff (rather than more effective organisations). While these are not mutually exclusive, companies need to determine the primary objective of organisation change initiatives and to escape faddism; consulting tools should not be part of a fashion industry.

Consulting is a Competitive Economic Game: "Eat or Be Eaten"

Over-promising by the consultant at the entry stage is partly driven by the "eat or be eaten" scenario. A colleague recently discussed a contract to work with a medium-sized Irish organisation.

The Issue: High labour turnover was leading to a haemorrhage of talent in a specific category. These people were difficult to hire/replace, with an estimated "loss" of £7,500 per person leaving.

The Brief: Understand the underlying reasons and recommend organisational solutions to reduce labour turnover from 15 per cent to 4–6 per cent in the next 12 months.

The Terms: Three consulting days (i.e. less than the cost of replacing *one* technician).

He had the guts to turn it down because it was impossible to do justice to the complicated brief in this timeframe. However, consultants have to be fairly secure to turn down work. The moral high ground can be a lonely place. Some companies want a hand-painted masterpiece but only wish to pay a photocopy price. Inevitably, trade-offs on quality are made and those managers who compliment themselves on their negotiation skills by getting lower cost consulting may be buying low quality service.

How Much Should You Pay a Consultant?

In the same way that there is a price for double-glazing, there is a market price for management consulting. Within the consulting profession, there is also a very definite price hierarchy. Where the consultant figures on the price ladder will be determined by their particular skills, their substitutability and their clients' willingness to pay the fees requested.

Deciding on the actual level of pricing is more art than science. In early 1991, I had a conversation with a US consultant, Bob Gattie, on pricing. His tongue-in-cheek advice on "pricing" ran as follows: "When a client asks you how much you charge you should immediately state the highest possible number you can think of without laughing". In similar vein, another US consultant, Professor George Yip, told me his ambition was to work "half the days at twice the rate".

Humour aside, the pricing issue is interesting in that it helps the consultant to define "where they are" in the marketplace. What consulting league do they wish to play in (Premier versus Third Division)? What skills do they have? What is their "unique selling proposition"? Some consultants boast about "high daily billing rates" — but this does not always translate into a high income. Others under-price their time and end up frazzled (150–200 mile overnight drives between assignments, etc.). Ultimately the consultant must determine a rate which provides the income they require and which their clients feel comfortable with — not just as a "once-off", but on a continuing basis.

From the client's perspective, the hiring manager needs to be comfortable with the daily cost and the projected total cost of the assignment. Useful questions include exploring the billing rates with other clients, who pays if there is an overrun on time, etc.

Moving the Focus from "Cost" to "Benefits"

Price can sometimes be an early "sticking issue". Some clients, on learning the daily billing rate, automatically multiply this by 365 (days in a year), contrast this with their own salary and mentally determine that the price is too high! The consultant has to help the client see that measurement of consulting is not just a cost issue — they need to focus on the "added value" (see model below).

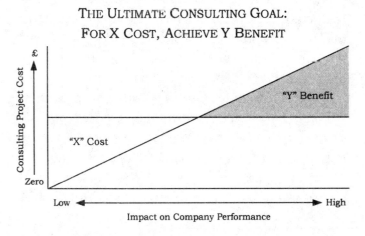

THE ULTIMATE CONSULTING GOAL:
FOR X COST, ACHIEVE Y BENEFIT

This is also useful for the manager engaging the consultant, as he or she may well have to "sell" the benefits of using the consultant to an internal audience, who may well be sceptical of the benefit of doing this.

On a personal basis, when I worked as a Personnel Manager I had experience at both ends of the cost spectrum — with terrific consulting advice that cost £3,000+ per day and some terrible work completed for 10 per cent of this rate. Ultimately, the quality of the work is usually remembered long after the price is forgotten. The cost versus benefit idea is illustrated in the story below.

InsuranceCo:[2] *The Rural Branch Office*

In 1995, we became involved in a small project in the insurance industry. A branch office in a rural location was under-performing significantly vis-à-vis sister offices of comparable size, catchment area, etc. A key element in the problem was a relationship issue between the branch manager and the "Number 2". This "chemistry problem" had been going on for some 15+ years and the staff had divided into two camps.

I visited the offices for two days and met all of the key personnel. I eventually worked out six options to move the situation forward — along with the upsides and downsides of each option.

Within a couple of weeks, the company had decided to go with one of the options detailed. A

---

[2] The company name has been changed to protect confidentiality. This applies to all of the examples used throughout this book.

manager retired early and several initial transfers were made. The branch is now performing in the premier division within that particular organisation and all of the key personnel issues are now resolved.

- Consulting Cost: £6,000

- Benefit: *Resolution of 15-year-old problem; significant performance improvement since then.*

While it is not always as easy to "ring-fence" the specific costs versus benefits, this example demonstrates how real organisation value can be added through consulting.

Be Crystal Clear on Billing

There is a social awkwardness around talking about money and many people swim away from this. However, confusion around billing can later lead to problems in the consulting relationship. For example, some clients feel that the first couple of meetings with a consultant are part of a "warm-up" ritual — an unpaid part of the proposals stage. This may even apply to the initial submission of documentation. If the client is subsequently billed for this "free time", it can damage the level of trust which underpins every effective consulting relationship.

Question: When is a Job not a Job?
Answer: When it's a Freebie!

The consultant needs to be crystal clear with clients on what time they are investing in a project and whether this time is billable or part of a "getting-to-know-you" exercise. The consultant also should be clear whether the rate quoted is an estimate or a "not-more-than" figure. Some potential contracts get killed at birth because of misunderstandings around billing. Consulting is a high-trust game. Misunderstandings around money damage the level of trust and usually lead to the premature death of a client–consultant relationship. I should know, as I've messed up in this particular area at least twice.

The Future of Human Resources at DrinksCo

A large drinks manufacturer asked us to work with them on developing their future human resource strategy. As part of the "front-end" of this, we developed a listing of trends, an A–Z of emerging practices in human resources. The company thought that the work was a "free-front-end", a way for our company to get more business from them at a later date. I thought we were getting paid for this specific job. We eventually split the difference and agreed 50 per cent of our normal fee. Both the client and I felt that we were right.

On reflection, it seems stupid that there could be confusion on such a fundamental issue (i.e.

whether we were getting paid or not). Part of the problem is the difficulty in talking about money. Because of this, both the client and the consultant often collude in avoiding the subject. In other cases, where consultants are less well established, they can be apologetic about fees and seek to "avoid" this topic for fear that the client might not go ahead with the project. Being crystal clear on billing is part of effective contracting, which in turn is the cornerstone of effective consulting. The key questions that need to be addressed at the contracting stage are detailed at the end of this chapter.

Face to Face: Managing the Initial Meeting

The initial contact between consultant and client is a critical point in the consulting cycle. It includes setting up the first meeting as well as exploring what the problem is, whether the consultant is the right person to work on this issue, what the client's and the consultant's expectations are and how to get started. Usually, the client has two concerns at this point: (a) substance and (b) relationships.

Concern 1: Substance

Substance is the cognitive part of a discussion between the consultant and the client. The client presents a certain organisation problem (e.g. the need for training to improve the skills of people in a particular area). Substance is the rational, problem-solving part of the discussion, where "hard" and

often quantifiable aspects of the problem or issue
are dealt with. At this stage, the client essentially
asks, "Does this person have anything to offer?"

*The prior assumption is that the consultant knows
something about the area*

The foundation for consulting is defined expertise is
some particular area. Consultants usually have
some expertise around the problem or presenting
issues, as put forward by the client. Normally, it is
only after acquiring some technical expertise that
people start consulting. If the consultant doesn't
have some expertise, then clients will not ask for
their advice! Consultants can convince a client that
they have something to offer by:

a) Highlighting their own expertise/experience/
   education; or

b) Discussing previous consulting assignments where
   they tackled similar issues.[3]

Concern 2: Relationships

To function with people, consultants generally need
to have reasonably well-developed interpersonal
skills. This includes the ability to put ideas into

---

[3] Great care needs to be taken to protect client confidentiality. An attempt to impress a new client with "war stories" is
not simply unethical but runs the serious risk of convincing
the client that their confidentiality won't be protected. Maintaining confidentiality is a critical element of the "high trust"
relationship noted earlier. It is not something that features at
a particular stage but is more a way of working throughout
the consulting cycle.

words, to listen, to give support, to disagree and to maintain relationships. Relationships are built on interpersonal feelings and perceptions — the "softer" side of the interaction. During the initial meeting, both consultant and client are generating and sensing their feelings about each other. At this stage, the client essentially asks, "Can I do business with this person?"

Being Authentic is a Core Ingredient

Client: "2 + 2 = ?"
Consultant: "What sort of figure did you have in mind?"
We have found that, from the consultant's perspective, a core ingredient in successfully managing the entry phase[4] is authenticity — openly addressing the issues, how the client feels about these, their individual role to date in attempting to resolve the problem and expectations about the consulting relationship. Where there is any "fudging", with key issues of substance or relationships left unspoken, this damages the effectiveness of the consulting project. Obviously, being authentic is subject to the normal social conventions about "degrees of openness" — but the balance of advantage is to err on the open side. We can illustrate this with a specific example — which happened at the front-end of a new client relationship.

---

[4] Authenticity is an issue throughout the consulting relationship. We make several references to this key point later.

The Importance of Courage: "Squaring-up" to Difficult Interpersonal Issues

What does the consultant do when the central problem identified relates to the client who hired them? Sometimes a short diagnosis highlights that the client is the central player in the issues identified. It requires considerable courage for the consultant to present this, particularly when a relationship is new.

The Good News is We've Discovered the Problem: The Bad News is: "It's You"

The best example I have seen of this was when working with another Irish consultant who has a reputation for being particularly "authentic". We were working on a joint project in a city in rural Ireland. Following our first visit, we discussed the issues on the long train journey home. We both came to the conclusion that the managing director was a central player in the problems presented. The following day, the other consultant (who was leading the project) wrote to the managing director highlighting our concerns and clearly identifying the central point — that in our view the MD himself was a key part of the problem. If he was not prepared to discuss/modify his behaviour as part of the solution, we would not go forward with the project. Excerpts from the letter are detailed below:

> *Dear X,*
>
> *I've captured my thoughts on structure on the attached pages. You'll see that the biggest problem in being definitive about the structure is the uncertainty surrounding your role and your career interests . . .*
>
> *(. . .)*
>
> *Finally [the letter concluded], I have to say that ever since I met your team they have been uneasy, uncertain and unhappy with your role. You seem to be both involved and uninvolved at the same time. The result has been a leadership vacuum. You have to resolve this matter and restore clarity to the structure and direction of activity on the site . . .*

In this particular case, the managing director agreed with the interim diagnosis and we went on to work successfully with this company for over four years. This outcome was particularly positive. I have occasionally used the same technique since with mixed results (it can be the shortest consulting contract in history!).

The central issue here is to remain authentic — with the courage to state your convictions openly and honestly — even if it means losing the business.

The Managing Director who Would Not Communicate with his Directors

In working with a financial services company on a communications project, we came across another classic example of the *client* being central to the problem. We had been working with the client to improve internal communications. After a number of one-on-one meetings with directors, we had developed a tentative communications process. The meeting would allow the senior team to critique the draft plan.

At the meeting, one of the directors wanted clarification on a rumour that the company was about to form a strategic alliance (cross-selling products) with one of the major banks. The managing director, looking straight at the director, said, "My advice to you is to read *The Irish Times* on Tuesday next." This real "in the room" incident allowed us to have a powerful debate on why internal communications processes (no matter how cleverly designed) will simply not work if the will to make them work does not exist internally.

Should the Consultant ever Walk Away from Potential Customers?

To "walk away from a potential customer" seems a strange suggestion, but there are times when it is necessary. For us, there are two rules of thumb around "walk-aways":

a) When the client has no real interest in doing business and/or

b) When the foundations for a successful project are not in place.

The consultant must be prepared to walk away from contracts if they do not believe they are "do-able". To begin a project that is not achievable is a waste of the consultant's time and the client's money. We can review each of these rules of thumb in turn, illustrating with specific examples of projects where we were approached by potential new clients.

First Rule of Thumb: Does the Customer Have a Real Interest in Doing Business?

Car salesmen use the phrase "tyre kickers" to refer to people who continually visit car showrooms to "see what's on offer" — but never move beyond window shopping mode. In engaging management consultants, some companies operate a slightly more sophisticated model of the same game. These essentially fall into three categories:

a) *Decoys*: Internal procedures within some companies (and within most of the public service sector) have a rule that commercial contracts should only be awarded following a competitive tendering exercise. Sometimes this is run clinically — with all contractors having an equal chance. Sometimes, individual consultants are asked to tender for business simply as "cannon fodder" — where the decision has already been made to work with another consultant. As proposals are unpaid, the consultant can end up spending valuable time writing proposals that do not generate any business (or income). Over time, consultants do get a little smarter at spotting decoys but they remain a hazard in the consulting profession.

b) *Desk-based benchmarking:* Some managers see
proposals and conversations with consultants as a
legitimate form of benchmarking — a way to tap
into industry best practice from the comfort of
their desk! It has an additional benefit — i.e. cost =
zero. In our early days, I made a number of
attempts to secure work with one of the large
supermarket groups. I met the training manager
several times and discussed the latest thinking
around Management Development Practices. I
submitted a comprehensive written proposal on a
specific training assignment, sent him a range of
articles on the topic and even spent several hours
in one store, shadowing the store manager to see
the operating environment at first hand. Net result:
Zero business. I learned subsequently that this
manager had a reputation of having conversations
with consultants, tapping into their thinking and
"re-packaging" this for internal consumption. In
relation to my own efforts to impress this manager
and secure business, I should have remembered
the advice given by W.C. Fields: "If at first you
don't succeed, then quit — no good being a damn
fool about it".

c) *We don't need it:* There are a number of companies
who simply do not use consultants. Sometimes
this is budget driven — i.e. in some low-margin in-
dustries, the scope for additional spending is light
(albeit good consulting pays for itself — but this is
not always an easy sell). In other companies, there
is a belief that consultants do not add value. In
relation to securing business with one company, a

well respected OD consultant remarked: "It's like trying to get feathers from a frog."

It follows that some customers simply won't bite, and it doesn't make sense to invest too much time in trying to engage these. Probably the best indicator here is whether a company uses consultants generally. Where an organisation has a track record of using consultants, this indicates that the culture is open to external expertise. If they never use consultants, the consultant will have picked up a useful piece of data about the company culture which may influence their decision on whether to pursue a specific contract.

Second Rule of Thumb: The Foundations for a Successful Project Need to be in Place

The second reason to "walk away" is where the foundation for a successful project is not in place; for example, the absence of energy to drive a change programme forward.

To help us manage large-scale organisation change programmes, we developed the "Managing Large-Scale Organisation Change" model (see next page). The model allows clients to understand the typical phases that should be followed and the type of issues encountered at each phase. It also helps us to determine if the "climate for change" is conducive to making real progress — a point we can now explore in some detail.

MANAGING LARGE SCALE ORGANISATION CHANGE

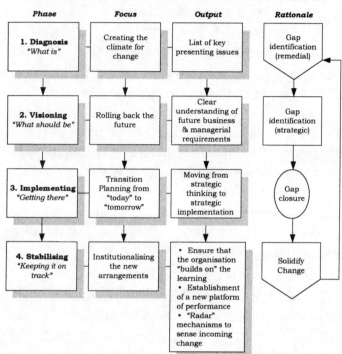

Phase	Focus	Output	Rationale
1. Diagnosis *"What is"*	Creating the climate for change	List of key presenting issues	Gap identification (remedial)
2. Visioning *"What should be"*	Rolling back the future	Clear understanding of future business & managerial requirements	Gap identification (strategic)
3. Implementing *"Getting there"*	Transition Planning from "today" to "tomorrow"	Moving from strategic thinking to strategic implementation	Gap closure
4. Stabilising *"Keeping it on track"*	Institutionalising the new arrangements	• Ensure that the organisation "builds on" the learning • Establishment of a new platform of performance • "Radar" mechanisms to sense incoming change	Solidify Change

The Twin Drivers of Organisation Change

A key point during "Phase 1" (the diagnosis) is to address the question "*Why* (are we doing this)?" Organisation change is normally driven by one of two motives:

a) *Vision inspired*: where a senior executive(s) has a clear picture of a "better tomorrow" and the personal energy to overcome the normal organisational inertia.

b) *Pain driven*: where the current performance is so bad that the situation is unsustainable.

A combination of clear vision, pressure for change and actionable steps ("what the hell should we do about this?") therefore provide the foundation for successful change programmes (see model).

REQUIREMENTS FOR SUCCESSFUL CHANGE[5]

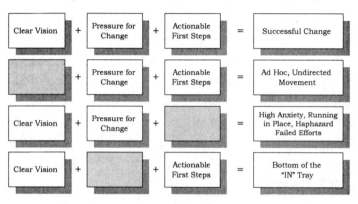

Sometimes change initiatives have elements of both patterns. In order to drive a change programme forward, companies often need to construct a clear "vision" of tomorrow — something which is significantly better than that which currently exists and which legitimises the short-term pain of the immediate changes required. In addition, successful change programmes often highlight the external pressures for change (market conditions, technology improvements, etc.), to convince a sceptical internal management or staff group that the changes are not "an optional extra" which the company can choose on an

---

[5] Original model developed by Professor Maurice Saaid, Insead University.

à la carte basis. In essence, the goal is to make the "wolf" more visible to provide the energy for movement.

Is there Enough Energy to Drive the Project Forward?

In the absence of significant evidence to support a "pain-driven" or "vision-inspired" initiative, a consultant should consider walking away from a change programme, as it is unlikely to go anywhere. Otherwise, they risk beginning an exercise (and soaking up clients' money) on a project which is unlikely to be completed. It may also damage their reputation as an effective consultant. We can illustrate this point with some real-life experience.

Changing Tracks:
The World Bank Railway Project

We were involved (as part of a wider consulting group) in a major Transport Project in Asia funded by the World Bank. The World Bank provides funding to developing nations, often supporting infrastructure projects (telecommunications, shipping, rail/road networks, etc.). By their nature, such projects are large and complex. In this specific example, an Irish consulting group which specialised in improving rail networks had secured the technical contract; PMA Consulting were asked to support in the area of "Institutional Development" — essentially the "organisation development" piece which would provide the glue for the technical changes being recommended by the technical consultants.

I well remember my first impressions on arrival in the particular country. It was incredibly hot (100°F) with over 90 per cent humidity. The group of technical consultants had been working away for about four months and there was great frustration that the project was going nowhere. Meetings scheduled with the local managers would be cancelled at the last minute. Interim reports submitted would be politely (but resolutely) ignored. The consulting group had no secretarial support and were housed in the single worst office accommodation I had ever seen. During my own time living in Asia I had come across poor infrastructure — and was quite used to a lack of "sophistication" in particular countries. However, this was of a different order; there was something more going on here.

Over the next couple of days I met with a group of senior executives in the client organisation and took them through the usual line of questioning (how well the project was progressing versus their expectations, their impressions of the consulting team, etc.). I also met individually with each of the consultants and worked through a broadly similar agenda. Less formally, we spent each evening together in a "consultants' bungalow" discussing elements of the project. Slowly, the "fog" started to clear.

The visit to the forgotten library

After about five days of trawling, an idea began to emerge. I discovered that the organisation had a library and asked if I could visit. The request to visit the library was deemed strange — but acceded to. The library itself was housed in an annex to the main HQ building. It did not look like it was overused.

In the clients' library I found three previous diagnostic reports, from UK, French and US railway consulting groups. Each of the reports covered broadly similar territory to the brief which our team was focused on. In terms of structure, content and presentation, at least two of these reports were world-class, certainly on a par with anything that the Irish consulting team would eventually produce.

Somewhat confused as to why the previous recommendations had been ignored and why we were on a "Xerox Mission" (a duplication of what was already in place), I discovered an interesting story. Access to World Bank money comes with a rider. You cannot simply get payment for the 60 locomotives or 60 miles of road (or whatever) without an addendum of foreign "expert" consulting support. In many cases, this is politely accepted as part of the package and politically ignored, much as you might discard the packaging of a new electrical item purchased for your home. I was now part of one such "packaging consulting team" and we were certainly being ignored. The likelihood of any real engagement with the local executive team seemed extremely poor.

In my report — prepared before I left after a two-week stint[6] — the following points were made:

Institutional Development: Current Status

- *If X Railways is to meet its goal of becoming a fully commercial railway operator, significant Institutional Development changes will need to be made. Stated more forcefully, without significant Institutional Development, the notion of effective, long-term change to a commercially oriented organisation will remain aspirational but will not become a practical reality. While some performance improvement is possible under the existing organisation structure and institutional arrangements, these are limited in scope.*

- ***The Central Problem:*** *The central problem to be addressed is a lack of belief within the executive team that the move to a commercially focused operation is possible. The fact that several previous studies have not been implemented is evidence that the current organisation is "frozen" . . .*

The problems at X Railways do not result from a lack of individual managerial talent. Taken together they represent a lack of collective political and managerial will to address the central issues

---

[6] The "shortness" of the contract highlights a key consulting dilemma. How do you "stay" with a contract for long enough to understand "what's happening" and "what's needed" while minimising the cost of the consulting assignment? It's a difficult balance to get right.

*confronting the organisation. As it currently oper-
ates, X Railways as a "whole" is less than the sum
of the individual parts. There is a need to openly
address the real problems faced and demonstrate
the courage to set and meet modern railway performance standards . . .*

*Without a fundamental commitment to tackling the
root causes of these underlying problems, the likelihood of successful, large-scale change at X Railways is poor and the organisation will continue to
inch forward.*

- **Suggested Next Steps:** *A series of interventions
  will be devised where the Railway Board, relevant
  political, governmental and railway personnel develop a crystal clear mandate for X Railways.
  Essentially this will address whether the management team are empowered to make the following type of decisions:*

  a) *Close loss-making services (while it is recog-
     nised that the railway has a public service ob-
     ligation, this needs to be defined with much
     more precision than is currently the case).*

  b) *Charge Fares/Freight rates in line with a
     normal market economy — subject to agreed
     public service obligations.*

  c) *Develop a network and service patterns where
     trains stop only at commercially viable loca-
     tions.*

d) *Source additional equipment as needed using a range of funding options (leasing, strategic customer contracts, etc.).*

e) *Make managerial decisions in relation to the timetabling of freight movements.*

The outcome will be the development of a clear national transport policy, which is not simply an extrapolation of past plans but sets out a realistic agenda for change. This will lead to a new institutional relationship between the government and X railways which will have the force of law.

Did it make a difference? I don't think so, chiefly because the political will was not in place to move that organisation forward. However, the Irish consulting team did get a "second project" extension and continued to work with the organisation for some time. Maybe the climate changed . . .

Putting the "Dead Cat" on the Table: Tackling Difficult Interpersonal Issues

During my first year in a consultancy role, I became involved with a New York[7] based publishing company. The managing director was a quite exceptional man. Brilliantly clever, he had a panoramic understanding of the industry and an

---

[7] Location/Industry has been changed to protect confidentiality.

ability to connect seemingly disparate pieces of information into a whole. He was also an alcoholic and managed the business through roller-coaster mood swings.

I had been working with the company on a number of small projects and had myself been on the receiving end of his changes in mood. Sometimes I was a "hero"; at others I was "an overhead which was not adding much value". Eventually, the marketing manager broached the problem with me using the memorable phrase "We have to put the dead cat on the table". She described the management meetings as taking place in a room where there is a "dead cat" (the alcoholism problem). "We can all smell it — but no-one wants to refer to it."

In many organisations, managers shy away from issues which are socially awkward; there are varying degrees of taboo around particular issues. Sometimes this is as it should be. In social situations, 100 per cent "truthfulness" would be way over the top and would inhibit normal functioning ("I see that you are putting on a lot of weight" might be truthful — but is unlikely to be helpful). However, there are times when the painful reality of bad behaviour needs to be addressed or confronted directly. When the source of the behaviour is the client, consultants need courage to openly address this. In this specific case, the outcome was quite positive. Confronted with the specific problem, the managing director agreed to seek professional treatment, which proved suc-

cessful; he continues to be brilliant — minus the mood swings. While such interventions don't always have a positive outcome, dysfunctional behaviour needs to be addressed. Where they are not addressed, companies generate unhealthy work climates and even mental illness.

The Body Odour Problem:
Don't Collude with Clients to Avoid Issues

On numerous occasions we have been asked to "collude" with clients to avoid personality/ behavioural issues. One memorable case concerned a mid-level manager who had a severe body odour problem. The problem was acute and caused significant discomfort for the people who worked near the individual. His peer group had tried the "softly softly" approach. However, despite numerous roundabout conversations about "daily showers" and the merits of specific antiperspirants, he did not get the message.

We were working with the client on an unrelated project, helping them redesign their organisation structure. The managing director, in a flash of inspiration, came up with a "two-birds-with-one-stone" solution. He suggested that we redesign the organisation in a particular way — the net effect being the physical movement of the individual concerned to an annex building. In this way, he would be isolated from the rest of the staff — "sent to Coventry" on the basis of his body odour problem. We refused to go along with this plan. However, we did spend time with the person's immediate manager — coaching him to confront the problem directly.

Sadly, in this case it was not a "Happy Ever After" ending and the problem continues to this day.

Contracting: Where to Start?

One of the most common consulting dilemmas is "where to start". Client companies who approach consultants will have a history and a presenting problem. Sometimes clients are at the initial stage (a greenfield consulting assignment where nothing definite has been progressed). More often, a series of initiatives (either successful or unsuccessful) will already be in place to address the issues presented. While most consultants would prefer the greenfield scenario, the reality is that, in medical parlance, "you have to take the patient from where he is, rather than from where you would like him to be"!

It follows that there is no "consulting sequence" or roadmap which fits all circumstances and no simple answer to the question "Where do I start?". As with all consulting assignments, you begin with a set of questions rather than answers. A good place to start is a review of the two core organisation questions.

Diagnosis: The Two Central Organisation Questions

In trying to understand any organisation (or sub-section) two key questions predominate:

1. What is the purpose of this organisation (unit, department, etc.)?

2. How well is it performing against this purpose?

Building a set of questions around these two central ideas will usually yield fruit, allowing the diagnostic process to unveil the relevant organisation issues.

"À la Carte": Selecting from a Predefined Menu

Another way to consider the question "where to start", is to review a roadmap of possible organisation intervention points. This can help to focus your thinking on those areas that are likely to yield results. We have developed a model for this (see "Organisational Change Levers" on the next page) which saves "reinventing the wheel" each time we work with a new client. Working through the model with a new client can help the consultant narrow down the area of focus and to agree the scope (what's in/ what's out) of an assignment.

ORGANISATIONAL CHANGE LEVERS:
"WHAT SHOULD WE WORK ON"

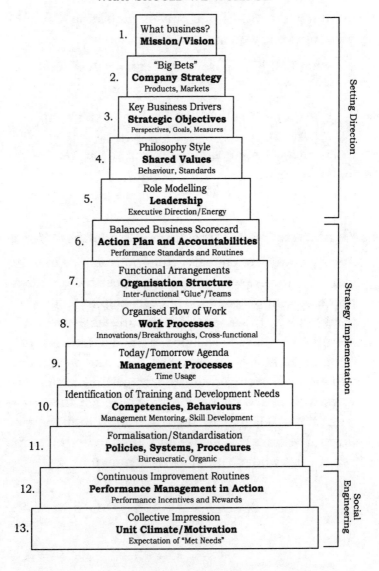

Is the Contracting Phase Different for Internal Consultants?

Theoretically, I don't believe that there is any major difference between internal and external consultants at the contracting stage. In practice, however, it can be more difficult for internal consultants to clearly agree the process in which they are engaged (whereas a written proposal or subsequent letter of acceptance from an external consultant is much more the norm). It may be useful therefore for internal consultants to mirror what happens externally — by formally agreeing projects/clarifying expectations — but not *too* formally.

We witnessed one internal consultant handle this inappropriately. On being appointed as an "Internal Change Manager" he attended a consulting skills programme in the US and took the contracting phase "into his blood". On return from the programme he would not meet with any internal managers (his peers) without a formal appointment. Prior to each meeting, he would e-mail them with his expectations for the session. Subsequently he would issue a formal "contract" to them on how they would progress the agreed topic. Most of his peer group found this method "way over the top". His interventions were eventually dismissed and he returned to a line management role.

The entry phase can occur throughout the contracting relationship as the consultant meets new groups of internal people. It is not a "once off" at the front end of the relationship. A useful summary of the key contracting issues is detailed below.

Key Contracting Questions

The following model[8] provides a useful summary of the key questions that need to be addressed at the contracting stage.

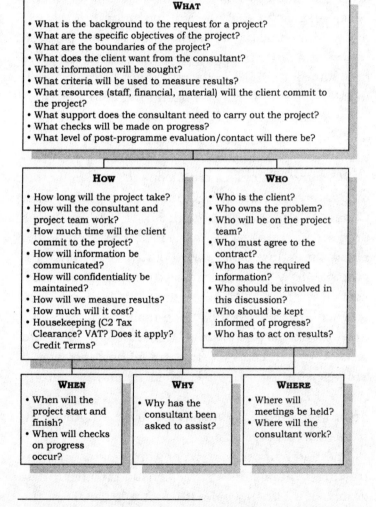

WHAT
- What is the background to the request for a project?
- What are the specific objectives of the project?
- What are the boundaries of the project?
- What does the client want from the consultant?
- What information will be sought?
- What criteria will be used to measure results?
- What resources (staff, financial, material) will the client commit to the project?
- What support does the consultant need to carry out the project?
- What checks will be made on progress?
- What level of post-programme evaluation/contact will there be?

HOW
- How long will the project take?
- How will the consultant and project team work?
- How much time will the client commit to the project?
- How will information be communicated?
- How will confidentiality be maintained?
- How will we measure results?
- How much will it cost?
- Housekeeping (C2 Tax Clearance? VAT? Does it apply? Credit Terms?

WHO
- Who is the client?
- Who owns the problem?
- Who will be on the project team?
- Who must agree to the contract?
- Who has the required information?
- Who should be involved in this discussion?
- Who should be kept informed of progress?
- Who has to act on results?

WHEN
- When will the project start and finish?
- When will checks on progress occur?

WHY
- Why has the consultant been asked to assist?

WHERE
- Where will meetings be held?
- Where will the consultant work?

---

[8] Taken from Charles J. Margerison (1988), *Managerial Consulting Skills: A Practical Guide*, Gower Publishing Co. Ltd. The original model has been modified.

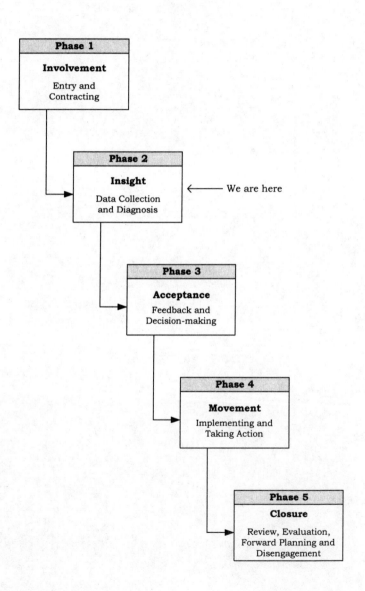

| Phase 1 |
| **Involvement** |
| Entry and Contracting |

| Phase 2 |
| **Insight** |
| Data Collection and Diagnosis | ← — We are here

| Phase 3 |
| **Acceptance** |
| Feedback and Decision-making |

| Phase 4 |
| **Movement** |
| Implementing and Taking Action |

| Phase 5 |
| **Closure** |
| Review, Evaluation, Forward Planning and Disengagement |

Phase 2

Insight
Data Collection and Diagnosis

> **The purpose of the data collection and diagnosis phase**
>
> 1. Collect enough information to understand both the symptoms (sometimes referred to as the "presenting issues") and the underlying causes.
>
> 2. Understand the climate in which the recommendations will be received.
>
> 3. Deal with resistance of the client to the consultant (initially in sharing information).
>
> 4. Collect and analyse data accurately and objectively.
>
> 5. Reduce the data collected to a manageable number of "issues".

When a consultant finally secures a contract, they are in position to collect data, i.e. to construct their own assessment of the situation. Helping clients to understand the "importance of understanding" can be a key part of the consulting role. However, any mention of the term "diagnosis" or analysis will cause the eyelids of some clients to droop. The old jibes about consultants suffering from "analysis paralysis" or "getting paid to tell us what we already know" underscore this point. Yet good data collection is a critical step in effective consulting. If you went to a medical consultant, she could recommend "two paracetamol" or an "amputation". Either option could be valid — you just hope that the diagnosis has been completed correctly! So too with management consulting.

There are Various Ways to Collect Data: Choose the "Best Fit" with the Overall Project Objectives

There are a number of ways to collect data with pluses and minuses associated with each method (a full listing is detailed later). The consulting skill lies in choosing the most appropriate tool to fit the circumstances. An important point here is that the method chosen will not simply influence the data collection phase — but will resonate throughout the project. As a general rule of thumb, the more resistance you are likely to encounter at the *implementation stage,* the more *inclusive* you need to be in the data collection phase. We can probably best illustrate this with an example.

Organisation Restructuring Projects: Using Inclusiveness to Support Acceptance

Over a number of years, we have been involved in a range of "Organisation Restructuring" projects. It normally happens as follows: the managing director or members of the senior team are unhappy with some element of the existing organisation structure. Based on this they redraw the structure and announce the new configuration. Our involvement would be in a technical capacity — helping to bring the underlying principles of organisation structure and design to the surface — ensuring that these were adhered to in any new configuration.

At the "entry phase", we would explain our role to the company as follows:

> There are huge degrees of freedom here. You can have a "Tudor style", a "Georgian style" or a "Swiss Chalet style" organisation. However, just as there are several structural engineering principles in architecture (depth of foundations, thickness of insulation, etc.) so it is with organisation design. To ensure that the new organisation will work well, you must adhere to the fundamental principles in organisation structure design theory.

New Structures are often "Spat Out" by the Receiving Organisation

Armed with the goods (the underlying theory of organisation design), we worked with various management teams to redesign their organisations. However, on a number of occasions when we "broke cover" with the new organisation design, staff would reject this, often arguing that better alternatives existed. As there are few absolutes in this area, some of the arguments made would indeed be valid. The new organisation structure would often come under fire — with varying levels of dissension — depending on the particular organisational climate.

Of the range of potential organisation consulting projects that can be tackled, changing the structure is the most obviously political — resulting in clear winners and losers. To overcome the negatives in the "traditional" method (the arguments and debate that often follow the announcement of a revised structure), we began to experiment with a different process (albeit the *outcome* would often be the same).

Step One

i) The existing organisation structure would be graphically represented on a single (A1 flip chart sized) sheet of paper.

ii) All of the presenting issues in the existing structure would be recorded and subsequently agreed among the management team (i.e. agreement on the "faults" in the existing structure).

iii) At this stage the focus is on *structure* as (a) the "boxes" (reporting relationships) and (b) the "processes" (how well the boxes work together). There is no discussion around the third element of structure — the *people* who inhabit the boxes.[1]

---

[1] For a discussion on structure, see Paul Mooney (1996), *Developing the High Performance Organisation*, Dublin: Oak Tree Press.

Step Two

iv) A "structural hypothesis" (or several of these) would be developed. This sets out the redesigned relationships and the supposed benefits that will flow from this.

v) The management team critique this set of materials — playing with different concepts and configurations. From this intensive session, a new organisational design emerges that is far more robust (in the sense of depth of acceptance *and* alternatives considered) than the traditional method.

vi) In cases where there is a lot of dissension, the planning process might go through a further "final" loop — to iron out any implementation difficulties or indeed to involve a wider group of managers in the design process.

Is this just Management for Slow Learners?

The role of the consultant is often to highlight or suggest a method, process or route to achieve a particular objective. This focus on process can often have greater impact on the organisation than a narrower focus on outcome only. However, in some cases, particularly where the process suggested is complicated, some managers see this as "game playing" — the elevation of process over substance. In one memorable phrase, I was accused of promoting "management for slow learners". To some extent, this view has merit — in the sense that time is a precious commodity and any process suggested should be economical in the use of management time. However, there is a more subtle point here which can sometimes be missed — i.e. a slow "front-end" can lead to speedier implementation. It might be labelled the East versus West timeframes phenomenon.

The East versus West Timeframes Phenomenon

When I worked in Asia the system of management initially seemed incredibly slow and ponderous. Having spent over 12 years working for American multinationals in Ireland, I was conditioned to a reasonably fast-paced decision-making process; Asia seemed like the "slow lane". For example, if we wanted to buy a new tablet press in a pharmaceuticals plant that had the capacity to punch out more tablets per minute, it had to run through a bureaucratic sign-off system. This seemed way over-the-top compared with the Western model of decision-making which puts a premium on the use of time; such "low level" purchases would often be decided by a single individual.

For example, within Intel, managers are conditioned to quickly "cut-to-the-chase" — and get to AR (action required) status. Complex issues are "done and dusted" — speedily actioned in a seemingly endless flow of high-paced decision-making progress. However, the Eastern method of management has some benefits when the decision-making phase (front-end) is considered alongside the implementation phase (back-end). An attempt to capture this diagrammatically is detailed below:

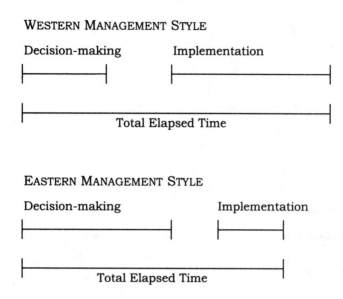

This insight has conditioned our general stance — with sufficient depth/emphasis being placed on the data collection and diagnosis phase so as not to move too quickly to implementation. It is a potentially useful point under a number of organisation headings.

The First Lesson in Psychology: People Don't Resist their own Ideas

The design of any consulting project needs to anticipate resistance and the best way to overcome it. In this sense, the "acceptance" question should be addressed at the project design (data collection) stage. It is generally not wise to completely by-pass the data collection/diagnosis phase on the basis that the elements of the problem are already understood. Allowing people to "reinvent the wheel" has the advantage that they eventually *own* the wheel; in organisations, "imported wheels" often lead to a bumpy ride!

We can illustrate this point by reference to one of the most interesting pieces of work we've completed in recent years — working with the Society of St Vincent de Paul to reformulate their Mission in modern Ireland. The front-end efforts at involvement were specifically designed to maximise the follow-through once the project was completed.

The Society of St Vincent de Paul: Mission Renewal

In 1996, we were asked to work with the Society of St Vincent de Paul. An international organisation, formed over 150 years ago to work with the disadvantaged in Paris, the Society has over 10,000 members in Ireland and is the second largest voluntary organisation after the Gaelic Athletic Association (GAA). Historically, the Society worked with the "poorest of the poor" — people who had hit a bad patch or who were socially excluded or marginalised in some way. In more recent years, their work has expanded into a range of areas and services outside of their traditional role and encompasses about thirty "separate" activities.

In 1995, the Society of St Vincent de Paul had an annual budget of £16 million. While this is a lot of money for a voluntary organisation, it pales into insignificance when contrasted with the annual spend of the Department of Social Welfare of £3 billion. One hundred and fifty years after the foundation of the Society, the Irish Branch had reached a crossroads with a need to reconsider their Mission in modern Ireland.

Because of the voluntary nature of the organisation, we needed to develop a data gathering mechanism that was inclusive. We decided to focus on the "Conference" level (essentially the local branches of the Society) — which typically had between eight and twelve members. Each Conference was sent a cover note explaining the overall project purpose and sequencing and asked to address the following questions:

1. *What are the key requirements of the people we serve?*

2. *What are our current strengths as an organisation?*

3. *What are our current weaknesses as an organisation?*

4. *Are there areas where we are not currently involved but should be?*

5. *How important is the spiritual dimension to the Society?*

6. *What is our fundamental purpose as an organisation?*

Pooling the data: From divergence to convergence

Responses were received from over 350 individual conferences and a number of individual members also made written submissions. From this mound of data a number of key themes began to emerge. These themes were debated extensively at the "Officer" level through a series of structured feedback sessions at which the initial reactions to the emerging data were recorded. Gradually, we began to piece the mission statement together.

More than a year and a half after our initial meeting with the Society, a Mission Statement emerged which captured the essence of the work completed by that marvellous organisation. This clarified that the organisation has three key strands that underpin their overall mission. This Mission Statement is reproduced as follows:

The Society of St Vincent de Paul: Our Mission

The Society of St Vincent de Paul is a Christian organisation, working primarily with the poor and socially disadvantaged. Our religious values are reflected through a range of actions in three key areas:

1. ***Immediate Support:*** *Through the relief of immediate suffering, we provide a confidential safety net for individuals and families in need. Respecting the dignity of the individual, we provide short-term material support and befriend those who are socially excluded.*

---

2. **Self-Sufficiency:** *We promote long-term self-sufficiency and independence through a range of self-help programmes. We seek to embrace those who are marginalised by society and help them to rekindle their self-respect and sense of worth. Where presenting problems are beyond our scope of competence, we build bridges of support with others more specialised.*

3. **Social Justice:** *We are committed to tackling the root causes of poverty in Ireland. The Society strives not only to alleviate need, but also to discover and redress the situations which cause it. Through the pursuit of social justice, we champion the rights of those we serve in a movement towards positive change.*

Our voluntary membership draws its inspiration in a union of community service and through the love of God.

By making significant "front-end" efforts to engage the membership of the organisation, the Society of St Vincent de Paul was able to get greater commitment to the final outcome.

From Industrial Tourist to Social Anthropologist

In addition to the inclusiveness = commitment issue, the Society of St Vincent de Paul project contains another lesson — the length of time needed to truly understand and work with an organisation. Why do so many organisational change programmes not produce organisational change? This question can, at least partly, be answered by the following assertion. There is a gross underestimation of the complexity of organisation design and behaviour and the change levers that underpin this. In order to develop successful organisation change initiatives, consultants need to stop working as "industrial tourists" and become true social anthropologists — linking with the "tribe" for long enough to understand what is happening internally, what historical factors led to "today" and what changes are likely to work in the specific culture.

Often in data collection there is a need a return to basics — to the roots of the social science method which has so much to offer business organisations. Great social science marries rigorous method with subjective feelings, values and judgement. However, too much of what passes for social science consulting is simply reductionism, soft science excellently marketed as a "one size fits all" solution. In working with client companies, we have increasingly encountered pre-packaged solutions masquerading as social science method. By definition, any organisational "solution" which is pre-ordained is unscientific. In practice, they often do not work, leading to "faddism" (flavour of the month) where a company tries numerous Band-Aid attempts to resolve core organisational issues.

In the short term, the movement away from the scientific method has a detrimental impact on the success of particular organisational change initiatives; poorly conducted organisational change initiatives simply do not produce organisational change. The longer-term impact is the creation of scepticism — the notion that social science has little, if anything, to offer the business world. Good consulting, which is focused on producing real organisation change and is not simply an income stream, has the potential to add true value to organisations and the people who daily live within them.

Taking it slowly in AviationCo:
The importance of "Depth" in diagnosis

In working through the consulting cycle, the normal sequence of events is that the client "presents" issues and asks the consultant to work directly on these. While, practically, this may be the only route forward, you need to be certain that you are "digging for oil" in the right place and that you have sufficient time to ascertain this.

The importance of depth of understanding was brought home to me when working with one particular client on a complex organisation problem. In 1994–95 I become progressively involved with a large company in the aviation sector. The initial contract was to run a seminar for the senior managers over three days. It went reasonably well and we began to work with the organisation on a range of change management initiatives.

One of the issues concerned under-performance by a particular group of "contract managers". The contract manager group were essentially project managers — a group with excellent personal tech-

nical skills and an encyclopaedic knowledge of the business. The presenting issue was that the performance goals set by the company were consistently "off target". Specifically, the company felt that the group was "caving in" to customer requests for additional services and was not generating sufficient revenue to support the business. The task: maximise revenue from customers by billing them (legitimately) for 100 per cent of the services they received.

It was difficult to determine the final price

This business was complex, in that the final price could not be determined until the customer's equipment was on site and received a detailed inspection. While estimates were given to customers in advance of the on-site inspection, these often proved conservative (price pressure from competing organisations trying to secure the same business forced "conservatism" into the estimation process). Often having secured a poor contract price, the expectation was that the contract managers (the on-the-ground managers responsible for doing the actual work) would maximise revenue collection — essentially through good negotiation skills around "extras" which emerged during the equipment maintenance period.

Complicating this arrangement, a customer representative maintained an on-site office for the duration of the contract. He had the diametrically opposite brief to the contract managers — to keep costs as low as possible and to get the maximum amount of additional work completed without in-curring any additional charges for his company.

The problem of underperformance versus expected revenue targets had been discussed several times with the group of contract managers. On two specific occasions, written clarification was given to the group to copper-fasten the senior management expectations around maximum reve-nue generation. Despite these efforts, the problem simply would not go away.

The working assumptions made were incorrect

Faced with continued underperformance, the executive team had to make some working assumptions as to why the additional revenue generation was not happening. Two central ideas underpinned their thinking; albeit these were not consciously discussed or documented.

a) The group of managers involved were not seen to have the commercial understanding or skills to effectively manage the operation. Training needs were assumed in relation to "economic literacy" (the revenue generation issue was key to the survival of the company and the manag-ers were not seen to fully appreciate the signifi-cance of this). In relation to skills, an understanding of effective negotiation tech-niques around the handling of "payment for extra services" was seen as a gap in their cur-rent "toolkit".

b) The group involved were not motivated. They were not seen to identify with the executives' team or the broader business objectives. Their orientation was to a narrow agenda — essentially doing business along the lines it had historically been managed (in a very different economic environment) when more "fat" (£) on the contract rates had masked a fundamental need to improve the baseline performance of the organisation.

Based on the above analysis, the group needed (a) additional economics/negotiation skills training and (b) to be "brought fully into the management net". We were asked to intervene and became involved in resolving the issue at this point.

The problem reappraised

Armed with this tentative analysis, I met with the contract managers' group and conducted in-depth interviews with each manager. I also spent three days "shadowing" one contract manager — literally following him from place to place over the course of three shifts, observing the pressures he was under and how he coped with these. During this time I was able also to observe the extent of the relationship with on-site customer representatives (a relationship which had remained in place for many years over a range of contracts).

Three central issues emerged from this analysis:

a) *There was an almost paranoid fear around airworthiness — which led to an overemphasis on managing safety (to the detriment of costs) — locally termed as "gold plating". While this was never formally tabled, it surfaced many times in the form of humour (e.g. "If something goes wrong you can't park on a cloud").*

b) *A huge pressure on turnaround time (the maintenance scheduling for aircraft put tremendous pressure on the client organisation to avoid "ground-time"). Aircraft sitting on the ground are not earning revenue. In some cases, significant cost penalties could be incurred if the maintenance was not completed on time.*

c) *Reduce costs: Chiefly by maximum utilisation of labour (e.g. low/no overtime) and charging the customer for all additional work and equipment/parts used.*

From this analysis, a revised problem statement emerged — one which recognised an inherent conflict in the role *(i.e. the problem was not one of individual skills or motivation but revolved around the job design itself). An attempt to diagrammatically capture this conflict is demonstrated on the next page.*

Once this role conflict was made "discussible" it was possible to move the debate forward — away from an unproductive focus on "what do we need to do to make the contract managers see the

*light" to "how can we best manage the inherent
contradictions in this role".*

Inherent role conflict:
Managing polarities/dilemmas

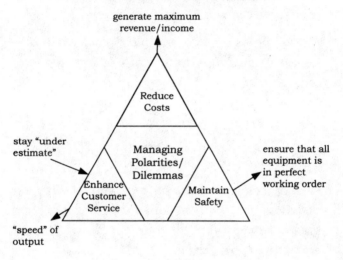

*The central point here is that a surface under-
standing of the issues did not reveal the true
source of friction or indicate how these issues
could be resolved. Indeed the surface diagnosis
had wrongly identified the central issues; spending money on "fixing" the contract managers was
not the route forward. The final diagnosis required
a depth analysis approach (i.e. several days spent
"shadowing" one of the managers) from which the
real issues could emerge. Some companies simply
will not invest this level of time or resources at the
diagnosis stage, seeing it as "analysis paralysis".*

"BankCo" Dilemmas: Managing Polarities within the IT Function

We were involved in a somewhat similar diagnostic exercise with the IT department of a company in the financial services industry. The presenting issue was that the IT department were "not delivering" and the relationship between the manager of the unit and his peers had broken down. We were asked to get involved and to "fix" the IT department. Similar to the example detailed in the aviation industry, what emerged was a role conflict issue; essentially, the IT department was being asked to deliver targets against several contradictory agendas (our attempt to capture this is reproduced below).

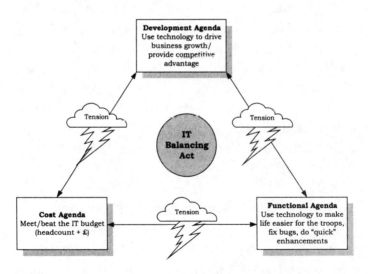

Key point: *Analysis is not instant; to really understand issues in an organisation usually takes*

*time and costs money. Without this investment,
too many companies put Band-Aid solutions in
place — over and over again.*

Grabbing Hold of an Instant Solution: Alleviating High Anxiety

One of the potential explanatory factors in the search for instant solutions is a release from anxiety.[2] Consulting projects tend to be highly complex and anxiety-provoking. By implication, the client is wrestling with issues which they do not know how to "fix" and which often cause unspoken feelings of inadequacy. The consultant, knowing little about the client's business, processes or culture, initially experiences similar feelings of confusion and anxiety. If the consultant proposes an acceptable "solution", both parties can escape these feelings in a fantasy that the issues are fully defined and the problem is on the road to being "fixed". In essence, clients and consultants collude with each other to escape complexity and the deep-seated anxiety that accompanies it. Faced with a choice between certainty and uncertainty, order and chaos — who would willingly chose the latter?

On Reflection: A Search for the Simplistic Solution

In the late 1980s, I worked as Industrial Relations Manager for a US multinational. Faced with indus-

---

[2] A small but growing body of literature is now developing around this idea — labelled "psychodynamics".

trial relations problems which seemed intractable (we had just come through a bitter month-long strike), we sought external counsel. I vividly remember the presentations made by a number of consultants to the management team. One consultant argued that he knew so little about the company that he would have to spend considerable time internally (to figure out the situation). He also made the point that OD programmes could not be totally pre-programmed in advance — that there would be a degree of ambiguity surrounding the outcome. Another consultant stated that the primary problem was "A, B and C"; that he had come across it on several previous occasions and that we would need to do "X, Y and Z" to fix it. Which advice did we buy? The latter, of course. On reflection, we were primarily buying comfort and hope — escaping our anxiety, becoming dependent on this external source of wisdom — a commercial "Jim'll fix it". We had entered into a contract with a beginning, middle and end (or at least the outward appearance of this). In practice, it proved lovely but as complex and messy as the first (unsuccessful) consultant predicted.

Trading off: Speed versus Depth

The arguments made above are that real understanding precedes solutions that work. However, in the real world, the benefits of speed versus depth need to be carefully weighted and sometimes it is wise to trade off speed of momentum against depth of understanding. Where a problem is particularly acute, you may not have the luxury of doing a "Full

Monty" diagnosis. In organisations, things will not stand still while you study them.

Even in larger-scale change projects, it can be useful to identify and progress some "early wins" (a Phase 4 initiative) — often to convince a sceptical audience that change is possible. The overall point is that as a consultant you cannot be purist in your approach to the data collection/diagnosis phase. The crafting of the intervention strategy needs to be tailor-made to the individual organisation and circumstances.

Using Speed to "Test" Managerial Commitment

In the mid-1980s, I attended a training programme at the Irish Management Institute. During one session, a presentation was made by two respected Organisation Development Consultants on their modus operandi. It was an early lesson on data collection and on testing management commitment. They told the following story.

Answer that Call:
The Telephone Exchange Contract

The consultants had been asked to complete a diagnostic study on a particular Telephone Exchange. The background to the project was a list of "personnel" type issues — absenteeism, lateness, low morale, etc. The consultants spent three weeks "living" in the Exchange and eventually produced a detailed report with a number of specific (50+) recommendations. Eventually, the phone call came through and they were asked to present their findings to the management team.

Wearing their best suits, they attended the meeting, hoping to get the subsequent job of im-plementing the report findings. They got a very different reaction — with the management team "nit-picking" a range of small issues ("recommen-dation No. 26 is in contradiction with No. 43"; "I notice that you continually spell practise incor-rectly throughout the report", etc.).

The consultants' working assumption was that the report would stand alone; i.e. it would be evaluated on the depth of intelligence which un-derpinned the recommendations. Yet they ignored a key point. Effective consulting is a highly politi-cal activity — not simply a technical/academic exercise in problem-solving. As we have seen ear-lier, no amount of consulting "brilliance" can over-come management inertia. In this sense it can be useful to use speed as a test of management commitment. Rather than a full-blown study, sometimes a short, sharp diagnosis is appropriate as a means to bring the real level of management commitment that exists to the surface and avoid the waste of time, energy and money detailed above.

The consultants said that after that experience they changed their modus operandi. They now conduct short, sharp diagnostic reports — reck-oning that they can highlight 80 per cent of the key issues in a couple of days. They then present this to a company in the form of a flip-chart pres-

entation (no bound, coloured reports). Depending on the management reaction, they then decide if the internal appetite is in place to allow them to go forward.

The "Psychiatrist Model": How am I Being Treated Here?

One useful concept during the data collection phase, from the consultant's point-of-view, is to ask the question: "How am I being treated here?" How they are treated (whether positively, negatively or neutrally) can indicate in a very concrete way the style of the organisation they are working with. Consultants should see the initial meetings/interviews conducted as a potent source of data — a "beginning" in understanding the problem. Asking, "how am I being treated here?" and "how do I feel about this organisation?" may provide an indication of how the organisation treats its staff or how the management team *feels* about working there.

The Non-union Plant:
Task Management "Par Excellence"

We were asked to do a small job (about 10 consulting days) with a large multinational company. The company is non-union and wanted to use a specific diagnostic tool that we had developed. The tool helps an organisation determine the strength of their positive employee relations stance and the likelihood of union encroachment.

The initial meeting with the management team began on schedule at 9.00 a.m. At 9.25 a.m. I was driving back to our office — business concluded. On one level, this was managerial efficiency personified; a reasonably complex planning session was "wrapped" in about 20 minutes and we had a firm commitment to "go ahead". However, on the way back to our office, trying to ascertain how I felt emotionally, a different picture emerged. It felt as if I had been "eaten up". A complex and important topic had been managed clinically and efficiently, but with little real understanding of the importance of the issues raised or empathy with the subject matter. It was if the managerial group had received an "A" on task and process — but a "D" on "feelings" or emotional content. Over time, that initial insight was to become a central kernel in the diagnosis of that particular company — in understanding how staff felt about working there.

How the consultant personally experiences a company is a key data collection mechanism, helping them to understand the reality of the workplace. The consultant's own feelings are an important barometer of the organisation climate. We call this the "psychiatrist model" — understanding what is happening in the room as an aid to a deeper understanding/diagnosis of an organisation and the specific issues being addressed.

Getting Creative: Using "Unusual" Methods to Bring Data to the Surface

Sometimes there is a need to develop an unusual or novel method to bring data to the surface. This can be useful if the issues involved are socially awkward (e.g. challenging a company's stated value system) or are difficult to bring up for some other reason. We can illustrate this point with a specific example.

"InsuranceCo": Installing a complex performance management system

In one large insurance company, we were asked to develop and install a performance management system. Conceptually, the managers wished to have a system in place that clearly identified goals and measured actual performance against them. However, data from our initial meetings with the management team indicated that it was unlikely that the company would support the installation of a performance management system for two reasons:

a) *The company had a 30-year history in which individual performance had never been measured; and*

b) *While the senior team "intellectually" supported the concept of performance management, we felt that, "emotionally", they were not 100 per cent behind it.*

Rather than simply present an assertion for which we had no solid evidence ("we do not feel that you really support the need for a performance man-agement system"), we needed some mechanism to make this "discussible".

The Debate Method: Are you For or Against Performance Management?

The method used to bring to the surface the lack of support for installing a performance management system was a formal debate. This revolved around the core rationale for the installation of a performance management system and allowed a group of managers to legitimately voice their objections to it. It was a "fun" event with a serious outcome. We set it up as follows:

Session Overview

1. *The management group was split into two teams. One team argued "for" and the other team "against" the following motion.*

   "Performance management is a waste of time. It is a paper chase exercise. It does not result in improved performance or behavioural change."

2. *Each team selected two speakers — a main speaker and a rebuttal speaker.*

3. *The team arguing "for" the motion spoke first for three to four minutes. They were followed by the "against" speaker.*

4. *The rebuttal speakers then had the stage for two minutes each.*

The debate brought a number of key concerns to the surface (list reproduced below). We were subsequently able to address these issues with the management team in the design of the new system.

Arguments "for" the motion

(i.e. performance management is a waste of time)

- *Too time-consuming*

- *Objectives simply state the obvious. Everyone understands their job.*

- *Objectives keep changing. System is too static.*

- *Behaviour/personality is a "fixed commodity". It cannot be changed.*

- *All managers have different standards. No system can overcome this.*

- *There is often a lack of a real company commitment to managing performance. A "system" does not equal commitment.*

- *Rewards are not commensurate with performance.*

- *Appraisal is a subjective process. Don't do it!*

- *It inhibits teamwork. Too individualistic.*

Arguments "against" the motion

(i.e. in favour of performance management systems)

- *Written objectives: Clarify goals.*

- *Two-way communication of expectations benefits both parties.*

- *Gets commitment to goals.*

- *Dynamic process. It can take account of changes.*

- *Gives sense of achievement. Links into individuals' need for self-esteem.*

- *Forces "face-to-face" discussions on a periodic basis — i.e. not just once a year.*

- *Links into training/career development.*

- *Links into rewards decisions.*

- *Helps control performance — i.e. early problem identification*

- *Provides organisational consistency. Defeats favouritism and subjectivity.*

Creative Data Collection Methods

Under this general heading, there are lots of options. At one training programme I attended in the US, Kirby Warren, Professor of Organisation Development at Columbia University, New York, advocated using the "legal" model for particularly important company issues. Where complex issues need to be decided, he suggested that separate management teams should be established to argue the case for the "prosecution" and for the "defence". The consulting skill is less in deciding the specific mechanism which should be used (there are so many options here) — but more in recognising the need to do something "outside of the box".

Who (Consultant or Client) Should Collect the Data?

The working assumption for many clients is that the consultants will complete the data collection exercise. However, it can be extremely useful for the client to be involved in this, with a local manager/team completing the data collection directly or shadowing the consultant. Direct client involvement in the data collection phase yields "richness" (an insider will have much more information than a consultant who is "cold from the street"). It can also signal organisational commitment — hooking the organisation at the front end in order to build commitment to the final outcome. In practice, it is difficult for managers to be "gung-ho" on implementation — if they do not agree with the prognosis.

The obvious downside to the direct involvement of the client in data collection is in the area of confidentiality. Sometimes it is useful for an outsider to meet with a group or individuals to promote a greater degree of openness in discussion (particularly where the issues concerned are socially awkward). As with many of the points made, there are few absolutes — the best method depending on the particular circumstances.

Stealing the Best Ideas Around: Benchmark Visits to Other Sites

Getting clients to conduct benchmark visits to other sites can be a useful part of a data-gathering exercise. For example, a manufacturing company in North County Dublin wished to introduce "team-working" into their plant. The manufacturing manager had come from a company in the west of Ireland that had a long (and successful) historical association with team-working. While personally "sold" on the concept, he was having trouble convincing his peers that team-working would add real organisational value; they would not simply be "discussion groups on the topics of tea, towels and toilets".

Through client contacts, we enabled the management team to visit three other manufacturing facilities which use team-working extensively. On the basis that "seeing is believing", these visits had much more practical impact than attendance at a seminar on the benefits of team-working or direct presentations by us trying to convince the management team that this was the route to travel.

Action Learning: An Old Idea with New Life

Benchmarking is very similar to the action learning approach pioneered in the UK over 30 years ago. Under the "action learning" umbrella, managers had to visit other sites (e.g. collieries) and observe what was happening there, and see to what extent the ideas could be applied in their own arena. The action learning approach can also be used by managers in a wide variety of situations. These include bringing managers together from different parts of the same organisation or bringing people from different organisations together. We have brought diverse groups (e.g. bankers and car sales people) together on a number of occasions to consult and learn from each other; the laboratory of real work is often the starting point for successful organisation change.

The traditional notion — that diagnosis is a one-way interviewing exercise conducted by consultants and resulting in the production of a "report" — is far too restrictive. There are a whole range of useful tools and approaches under this heading.

An Over-reliance on the "Survey Feedback" Method

A common problem at the data collection stage is an over-reliance on a single method: the survey feedback technique (from which the diagnosis is subsequently developed). This method involves the conducting of semi-structured interviews in the client company, which are then "fed back" in a report or presentation. The standard consulting joke about consultants "borrowing your watch to tell you the time" (and then keeping the watch!) is funny precisely because it is close to the bone.

Part of the explanation for the level of usage is the simplicity of this method of data collection. In other cases, it highlights a narrow "toolkit" of consulting skills. Some consultants have simply learned one method and are programmed to follow this, like robots in a car manufacturing plant specially adapted for one procedure. On the plus side, the survey feedback method has the advantage of producing order (because recommendations are usually funnelled into some priority ranking). Yet in organisational development projects, disorder is not to be kept at bay but entertained, encouraged and worked with — if this reflects the reality of that particular organisation.

Bottom Line: Good consultants have access to a *range* of data gathering tools and access these appropriately. Sometimes it's a screwdriver; other times a mallet is required (preferably a heavy one with a firm, rubber grip!).

Avoiding "Premature Revelation"

At the diagnosis stage, consultants can be put under tremendous pressure to "show their hand". Managers, impatient to hear the message, often ask: "What do you *think*?" It is quite seductive. Having recently arrived on the scene you may wish to demonstrate your intelligence by analysing what's happening and communicating this to the client. Generally, it is best to withhold this information for three reasons:

i) Firstly, it *is* premature. Before you finalise the data collection phase you may be dealing with a biased sample or simply be unable to draw conclusions. Giving an "update" at this point runs the risk of distorting the data or of watering down the opportunity of a later feedback session where you can make your central point to the combined management team. A clever way to highlight the "biased sample" idea is outlined over:

> It's   only
> when   you
> get   both
> sides   of
> a   story
> that   you
> truly   understand

ii) If the diagnosis is conducted *too* quickly it can offend the client — particularly if it is something that they have been struggling with for some time. Here again data collection is not simply an academic exercise — the clinical diagnosis of a particular problem — but part of a political process of getting commitment to a solution. It is certainly not an exercise in making the local management team look foolish (unless you want a "Pyrrhic victory" resulting in the shortest consulting contract in history).

iii) It may result in a foreshortened contract. When consultants "show their hand" too quickly, the clients might feel they have "got their value" from them, and contracts can be closed out prematurely (possibly a positive cost-saving device for clients).

iv) You may be in the "data dumping" phase and be overly negative about the organisation (see next point).

"Data Dumping": The Unburdening of Organisation Problems onto the Consultant

In organisations where personnel have not been well managed, there is a high possibility of "data dumping" on consultants. The process often works as follows.

Prior to conducting internal interviews, the consultant prepares a list of key questions. Inevitably, some of these are of the "what is not going well?/what do you not enjoy about working here?" variety. The combination of the forum (where it is legitimate to discuss negative topics) and a "sympathetic ear" (if local managers have ignored upwards feedback) can lead to an outpouring of issues. While this may be a perfectly valid explosion of fears/concerns/annoyances, the process accelerates this. The central point is that the degree of negativity can be considerably raised above the "norm" of frustrations felt.

In addition, some employees use this forum to "dump" on their manager (as a covert method of evening the score). Given the above, it is important for consultants to see the data collection phase in its wider context and not to be overawed by this.[3] It follows that, in compiling data, consultants need to be aware of the particular dynamics of this type of

---

[3] One of the interesting personal outcomes here can be a mild form of depression. Where back-to-back diagnostic sessions are very negative, consultants can "fill up" with this. It is important, in the write-up stage, to allow some time distance, which helps with perspective (good news/bad news), and also to try to factor in the importance of any recent events which may have coloured the feedback.

intervention and allow for this in providing balanced feedback to the client.[4]

ResearchCo:
If the client asks for "A" — give them "A"

My only defence for the following story is that I was new to the consulting game and extremely naïve on how the process works. In 1992, a client company in the UK asked us to conduct an identification of training needs analysis. The company operated a pharmaceutical research and development centre. Little formal training or development had taken place since its establishment, three years earlier. Our brief was simple. I was to look at the business, interview all of the key research scientists and come up with a draft "Training Plan" for the next 18–24 months.

During the data collection meetings, a number of "sidebar" issues emerged — chiefly around the interpersonal style of the MD himself. He was quite a character. Having come direct from academia, this was his first job managing others in a commercial operation. Armed with my audit information, I fed back to him the data collected —

---

[4] One of the enduring criticisms of consultants is that they "create problems which they subsequently resolve". Specifically, consultants are accused of making problems seem worse than they are in reality in order to create pressure on managers to resolve these. While this is obviously highly unethical — if done intentionally — my guess is that the potential negative dynamics of "data dumping" are not always fully understood by consultants.

including an amount of negative material on his interpersonal style. It went down like the proverbial lead balloon. Cutting to the chase, his summary ran as follows: "I asked you in good faith to do A. You've done B. Good luck with the rest of your consulting career."

Sometimes it is entirely appropriate (and adds real value) to present additional information to a client. In this particular case, I had not gained entry with this client to do anything other than a technical study on training needs and completely misjudged his likely reaction to the "management style" feedback. Armed with my own "cleverness", I lost sight of the client's needs. For him, it was the equivalent of going to a car mechanic and being criticised for his dress sense. Ouch! The general rule of thumb for every consultant is: "If the client asks for 'A', give them 'A'." However, sometimes you need to "steer" the client into another area — as our next case illustrates.

GlassCo: What do you do if the Client Wants the "Wrong" Product?

We were involved in an extremely interesting project in a city in rural Ireland. The client had requested our input to help them develop a "team-based" organisation.

Working with another consultant, we visited the plant and met with the Human Resource team and separately with the MD. We went through the company's plans, operating performance statistics and the specific objectives for the team-based initiative. Our role was to support the management team in installing this.

Driving back to Dublin, an idea began to form: developing a team-based organisation was not what the company needed at that point. Rather, they needed a mechanism that would both reduce their labour costs and involve the workforce. Some of the points made to the client are reproduced below.

Do staff really believe that change is necessary?

A key emerging question is whether staff understand and believe that change has now become a necessity. While we did not meet directly with any of the hourly paid group we would suspect that many people do not really believe fundamental/ radical change is necessary in Company X. Why?

- *The plant has a history of success within the corporation.*

- *High levels of overtime earnings are in place for over ten years and people interpret this as "the company is doing well".*

- *While there has been talk of increasing competition, there has not been any visible evidence to demonstrate this.*

- *The previous effort to involve staff did not work 100 per cent and there has not been a visible downside (life has continued as normal).*

- *The core rationale for the change (the movement to team-based working) is not visible.*

- *While the shop stewards' group have given a cautious welcome to the approach, this may be on the basis of a strategy of "wait and see what shakes out"; there may be a belief/expectation/ hope that the company is going to "pay for change".*

- *The plant is continuously in a "back order" position, sending the message "we are incredibly busy".*

Bottom Line: *We need to build a credible internal change message.*

Why do we believe that the movement to a team-based organisation at Company X (as a standalone initiative) will not be successful?

Perhaps we can illuminate with a story. What happened to the architects and builders of the pyramids? Inside the Pyramids, the pharaohs built intricate tunnels so that they could hide all their valuables for their new life. When the work was finished, everyone who knew about the tunnels was killed. When the pharaoh asked "are you nearly finished?", what were the builders going to say? Probably "Not yet."

The same basic logic applies to the hourly paid group in Company X. Asking people to suggest improvements ("How can we work smarter?") which will effectively decrease their overtime earnings is unlikely to be a successful formula.

Problem Statement

The organisation is currently faced with a management conundrum:

a) How can we reduce labour costs from 45 per cent to X per cent (to be specified).

b) How can we "turbo-charge" the performance of the hourly paid group, moving them beyond the simple calculus, "what's in it for me?"

In this specific project, I believe we managed to save the company a lot of money and emotional grief by reframing the problem from the installation of a team-based system towards one which dealt with the fundamental issues facing the organisation — i.e. labour cost reduction/lower overtime earnings.

Making Sense of it All: Dealing with Reams and Reams of Data

For me, the most awful moment in the entire consulting cycle comes at the "making sense" stage. You are sitting at a desk with 20 (or 200) A4 sheets of hand-written[5] data — contemporaneous notes from

---

[5] During the data gathering phase, it is possible to use a laptop computer and input data directly. My experience with this is that the technology acts as a sort of "invisible barrier" to the data collection process — reinforcing the businesslike nature of the meeting and undervaluing the human dimension. The same basic point applies to the use of tape recorders. For this reason, we find that data collection interviews are best conducted with "old" technology — pen and paper.

the data collection meetings. The moment of truth has arrived — how to make sense of it all! We use a simple two-step process to move forward at this point.

Step 1: Make a Skeleton Structure

Make a "skeleton structure" of your report — with all of the key headings listed. A typical structure might contain the following:

i)   Background to the study

ii) Key presenting issues

iii) Recommendations/discussion points

iv) Alternatives considered

v)   Implementation plan, obstacles and timeframes

vi) Investment costs

vii) Appendices (methodology, support data, etc.).

Step 2: Fill in the Details

Write up the individual key headings onto a series of A3 sheets of paper. Once you have decided on the overall structure, you can begin to "populate" the A3 sheets with the data from the individual interviews.

As a personal preference, I do this manually and only transfer the data onto computer once these initial two steps have been completed. This allows the interconnectedness of points to emerge somewhat more easily than switching through numerous computer screens — but this is a matter of personal choice.

Beyond Transcription: Analysing Data in a Way that Makes Sense to Clients

The data collection phase is not simply a mirroring exercise — reflecting back to clients what you've been told and "piggybacking" on the suggestions made by the management team. The belief that consultants offer limited added value — other than simply "capturing" issues that are already known internally — has been touched on earlier. Good data analysis goes well beyond this. Let's move again from theory to real life — this time to the electronics industry.

"ElectroCo": Making sense of confusing data

We were asked to conduct a diagnostic study in one large manufacturing plant in Ireland. The plant, recognised for its high productivity, was experiencing a significant shift in business focus and there was some "fallout" (morale problems) among the management population. We were asked to work with the management group in diagnosing what was happening and resolving it.

We designed a semi-structured interview and met with all (20+) of the managers in the particular section. Following these meetings we constructed a feedback report/presentation including the hypothesis outlined below.

What is the staff reaction to the ElectroCo culture?

There is no single managerial response to the ElectroCo culture. Essentially, the management group sub-divides into three camps (with most people in the "B" camp).

Camp A: This is the way it is (and I love it)

"This is a vibrant place to work"

"It is a tremendously exciting place to work —
it's never, ever boring"

"I personally feel very attached to the ElectroCo values"

This group are truly "sold" on the ElectroCo culture. Many of the people are able to directly quote the Chief Executive (i.e. "We come to work" — the Chief Executive's stated personal values) and have inculcated the ElectroCo values as their own. Many of the managers in this group have learned their trade at ElectroCo, having secured their first managerial roles here.

Camp B: This is the way it is (and I accept it)

"You can decide to be a leader or a follower. If you decide to be a leader, sign up for upsetting some people"

This group essentially believe that:

1. ElectroCo are great at A, B and C (hard stuff)

2. ElectroCo are poor at managing X, Y and Z (soft stuff)

3. I can live with X, Y and Z.

Many of the people in the B group are "converts" i.e. they initially moved from the "I hate this" position (see Camp C) and have now bought into the ElectroCo culture (on the basis of the total compensation package offered and the business results which have been achieved at the Irish site). However, feelings of being "in a fur-lined mouse trap"/ "golden handcuffed") are widespread.

Camp C: *This is the way it is (and I hate it)*

"This place has no soul"

ElectroCo have gone through a significant ramp-up period. During this time, the company have extended the number of production lines, subsequently downsized the plant and are now in transition into a new business — with more to come. People in this group are reeling from the pace of change. Some of the managers are exhibiting very high stress levels ("I'm totally exhausted"), with symptoms of clinical depression ("My life is out of control") and "learned helplessness" ("I've tried to fight the system but you continually get beaten down").

This analysis of the different "management populations":

i)   *Helped the company to make sense of conflicting data (e.g. feedback from managers in the A and C camps was confusing).*

ii) *Allowed the company to understand both the pluses and minuses of its current operating system in terms of the impact on management.*

iii) Allowed the company to craft a workable response to actually move the problem forward.

Telling the Good News: People Change from a Position of Medium Security

By their nature, diagnostic studies tend to be negative. They focus on the gaps in the current operation. When managers read through consultants' reports, they can react negatively to this. "Did they not find anything that was working?" is a typical response. As the purpose of the overall exercise is to get forward movement (as distinct from damaging the self-confidence of the management team), you need to find a way to table the "bad news" without switching off the audience. One useful mechanism to overcome this is to write a "good news" section in your initial report. This gives explicit recognition to the things that are working well and opens up the audience to receive negative or critical feedback in a more positive vein.

Dr Rick Gilkey is Professor of Psychology at Emory University in the US. Rick's central thesis (in relation to human change) is that "people change from a position of medium security".[6] The analogy here is one of a "mental castle". When people are feeling insecure, the drawbridge is pulled up tight as a form of protection. When they are overconfident, the drawbridge is also "up tight", this time as a result of arrogance. The ideal positioning is "medium

---

[6] In conversation with the author, May 1994.

security" — the confidence to take new information on board minus the arrogance of not feeling the need to change at all.

In conducting an organisation diagnosis, specifically identifying the "good news" allows this "medium security" positioning to be achieved. It is both an attempt to genuinely recognise the internal issues that are being managed well and provide a form of "sugar coating" which allows the medicine to become more palatable to the client. One specific mechanism to achieve medium security is a focus on what has worked well in the past — at the front-end of a management team agenda. A typical agenda that follows this format[7] is detailed below.

ORGANISATION PLANNING MEETING

> **1. Meeting Purpose: Today's Agenda**
> - Improve performance through an open examination of our current status vis-à-vis the installation of team-based working.
> - Build a united executive team with a common purpose.
> - Lay a "foundation of excellence" as a precursor to developing a truly world class organisation.
>
> We will consider this meeting a great success if . . .

---

[7] The topic addressed is installing a team-based organisation, but the same basic structure could be used with any topic.

2. Groundrules for the Meeting

- Consultants are always right!

- This is a secure environment. Both positive and negative opinions are OK. We left our positions outside the door. There will be no hierarchy in the sessions.

- Organisational change is a messy process. The discussions at this meeting will not be linear. Sign up for some frustration/confusion in advance.

- If it isn't both substantive (which at times probably means disagreeable) and fun it isn't worth the effort.

- Have the courage of your convictions and state any opposition openly during the meeting. Afterwards it's "disagree and commit".

Current Strengths

In relation to developing a team-based organisation, what are the current organisation strengths? What are we particularly proud of to date?

3. Moving Forward by Understanding the Past

Supporting a team-based culture: What have we not done well to date/would we change if we had the opportunity to relive the past 12–18 months? Do we still believe that the installation of a team-based culture is the best way to achieve a high-performance organisation (high productivity, flexibility, etc.)? Are teams the correct "tool" to achieve this?

4. Challenges Ahead: *What are the Key Presenting Issues at this Point?*

In terms of developing/installing a team-based culture, what are the big issues at this point? How should the issues listed be prioritised?

Moving forward by rolling back the future
Groups tasked with developing initial solutions to the key prioritised issues. Focus is on the "hard agenda" items.

Moving forward by being authentic about the present
How well is this management group working as a team? What is the feedback on some of the data collected to date? How can we move this forward?

Developing an outline project plan
What do we need to do next (e.g. the key projects that we will address)? How should we organise ourselves to accomplish this? What resources are required? Who else needs to be involved in this?

5. Communication to the Staff

Should we communicate the outcome of this meeting to the staff? How/when should we do this? What are the immediate next steps?

Are we Asking the Right Questions?

Usually before consultants meet a group of internal managers, they already have a good idea of the problem area to be addressed. This may have been detailed as part of a "briefing note" and will certainly have been spoken about during the "getting-to-know-you" meetings with the client. It follows that the target area is somewhat pre-set. At the data collection phase, I occasionally use a "prompter sheet" to ensure that there are no additional issues which the individual respondent/group would like to see addressed (as in the "A–Z Problem Identification Approach" below).

AN A–Z PROBLEM IDENTIFICATION APPROACH

A	Attitudes? Antagonisms? Apathy? Adaptability? Aesthetics? Automation?
B	Behaviours? Bottlenecks? Bargaining? Bureaucracy? Budgets?
C	Communication? Climate? Change? Crises? Complaints? Careers? Conflicts?
D	Delegation? Decentralisation? Defects? Danger? Difficulties? Deviations? Durability? Deadlines?
E	Environment (situation)? Economy? Errors? Ethics (morality)? Experimentation?
F	Frustration? Fear? Fantasies? Fun? Failure? Forecasting?
G	Garbage (as in computer inputs/outputs)? Goals? Group (processes)?
H	Hazards? Half-measures? Hierarchy?
I	Indecision? Interaction (inadequate, inappropriate)? Intentions? Insensitivities? Ideas? Ideals?
J	Job (design, enrichment, cycle, rotation, security)?
K	Knowledge?

L	Listening? Loyalty? Leadership? Lemons? Laziness?
M	Motivation? Money? Manpower? Material? Methods? Mix-ups? Meetings?
N	Negativism? Nit-picking? Negotiation? Needs?
O	Organisation? Objectives? Operations? Opportunities? Obstructions?
P	Pressures? Performance? Policies? Plans? Personnel? Procedures? Pay? Pessimism? Production?
Q	Quality? Quantity?
R	Resistance (to change)? Rejects? Reward System? Relationships? Responsibility?
S	Safety? Standards? Seasonal set-ups? Scheduling? Sales? Secretaries? Staff?
T	Training? Turnover? Time Management? Timing? Team (building management)?
U	Utilisation? Urban (aspects)? Union? Unity? Unification?
V	Vendettas? Venom? Variables? Visibility?
W	Waste? Workweek? Workday? Warehousing?
X	expense?
Y	Yesterday's breadwinners? You–I?
Z	Zero defects? Zig zags?

An outline of the most common data collection methods along with the advantages and limitations of each is detailed below.

COMPARISON OF COMMON DATA COLLECTION METHODS

Advantages	Limitations
Questionnaire Survey	
• Low cost • Anonymity • Respondent sets pace • Variety of options • Standardisation possible • Quickly processed • Easy to administer/no expertise • Can be administered to large groups	• On-job responding conditions uncontrolled • Return rate rarely controllable (75 per cent return is excellent) • Design is difficult • Usually some time lag for returns through mail system • Reliance on norms may distort individual responses
Observation	
• Can be non-threatening to participant • Objective	• Possibly disruptive • Reactive effect • Unreliable • Trained observers necessary
Interview	
• Flexible • Opportunity for clarification • Personal contact	• High reactive effects • High cost • Labour intensive • Trained interviewers necessary

Advantages	Limitations
Focus Groups	
• Very efficient means of collecting data from a representative group of respondents • The data may be richer because respondents can build one another's responses	• Data analysis may be difficult and/or confusing • Validity of data may be compromised by dominant individuals taking over the sessions
Documentation Review of Records	
• Reliability • Objectivity • Ease of review • Minimal reactive effects • Appears to be valid	• Lack of knowledge of criteria for keeping/ discarding records • Information system discrepancies • Indirect nature of data • Need for conversion to usable form • Sometimes expensive to collect
Benchmarking/Action Learning	
• Client involvement • Link with real world • High "impact"	• Transference difficult • Time consuming • Access difficulties

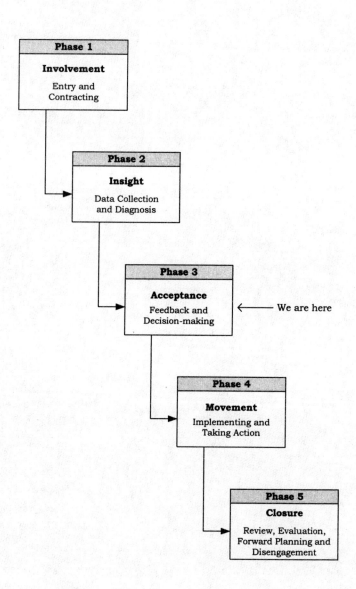

Phase 3

Acceptance
Feedback and Decision-making

---

*"The man who tells the truth should have
one foot in the stirrup"* — Turkish Proverb

The purpose of the feedback and decision-making phase

1. Authentically feed back data to the client.

2. Assess the client's reaction, including emotional response.

3. Deal with points of disagreement/concern.

4. Decide whether to move forward or disengage.

The data collection and subsequent analysis must be reported back to the client in a professional manner. During this phase, the consultant is almost always in the position of reducing a large amount of data to a manageable number of issues. The key skill here lies in sorting out the "important few" from the "trivial many". The consultant must avoid a tendency to feed *everything* back. Clients generally need a consultant to interpret or make sense of the data;[1] the confidence to do this grows in line with the consultant's experience. In our early days, anxious about leaving anything out, we fed back all the data. The usual result was to confuse the client.

Should the Feedback Data be Sent in Advance?

Once the diagnostic report has been completed, the consultant is faced with a dilemma. Should they send this in advance to the management team or wait and present it followed by a hard copy? The answer is (yes, you've guessed it already): "It depends." There are two contradictions that must be managed under this heading. Firstly, where time is short and the management team need to work through a lot of data, the core argument is that materials should be sent in advance and digested. The upside here is economy in the use of management time. The argument *against* sending the diagnostic report in advance is that written communication cannot be "managed". My experience is that reports, particularly those which highlight "gaps" in an operation, are best presented in person, followed by a detailed written report. The balance of advantages is therefore *not* to send the material in advance of the initial feedback meeting.

---

[1] For some "process consultants", this is a debatable point. The suggestion made would be seen to be overly prescriptive, i.e. with the consultant leading or directing the client. It links to the points made in the Introduction about "what is the appropriate consulting role".

From the Horse's Mouth: Using "Testimony" to Highlight Issues

A useful way to present data to an organisation is to use testimony. Testimony (what people actually say) is a very powerful feedback tool. Well chosen, pithy quotes can cut to the heart of the matter.

While individuals are often guaranteed confidentiality in the data collection process, any potential dilemma can be overcome by using actual quotes but making them anonymous.

Testimony helps to ensure that the messenger (consultant) is not accused of "creating the message". This is not a mechanism for consultants to hide behind but a way to table *real* concerns openly and honestly.

Being Authentic: Telling It As It Is

A key dilemma concerns the level of openness in which the issues are fed back to the organisation. Should the consultant "tell all" or does this risk damaging the confidence of the management team? Should some issues be held back and released later — a drip-feed method of bad news delivery? In making this decision, the consultant can return to a fundamental question: "What method will best satisfy the overall project objectives?" We can again illustrate with a specific example.

HealthCo: Taking the Medicine

We worked with one organisation in the mental healthcare field. The organisation demonstrated an astonishing level of care and compassion and had been doing so since the mid-1950s. They provided care to a truly marginalised group and historically had done so at a time when no-one else was even acknowledging the problem. However, in the intervening years a number of other organisations had come into the frame and were beginning to provide a competing range of services. These changes in the external environment, coupled with several internal issues around the empowerment of staff, essentially meant that continuing "as is" was not a realistic option for the organisation.

Despite the knowledge that some external organisations were now competitors and that the modus operandi for managing staff (in a more participative way) had changed significantly, it was proving difficult to get our client to move forward. We achieved this by using dissonance (see below), promoting change through the use of specific language that the leaders of that organisation could relate to. After completing a formal diagnosis in which care and development were developed as the twin elements of their mission, we gave them a "score" of "A+" for Caring and "D" for Development. Slightly incensed by such an overt low score, what followed was an open and highly

*effective dialogue about the need to reformulate
their core method of operating internally.*

Using Dissonance to Promote Change

As a generalisation, we can state that most organisations exhibit a degree of inertia. Organisations often become complacent about current performance
levels, particularly those that are doing well. In a
reverse of the common axiom, we suggest that "success breeds failure". If something has been done in a
particular way for over 30 years with no obvious
downside, the rationale to change is not obvious.

However, the factors that underpin success are
seldom stable over time. Organisations that do not
continually reinvent themselves are normally in the
"cross-hairs" of competitors, as captured in the Jack
Welsh quote: "If the rate of change outside your organisation is faster than the rate of change inside
your organisation, the time-bomb is ticking."[2] Organisational complacency (whether through arrogance, laziness or lack of management ability) is
seldom sustainable.

There are many Potential Reasons for a "High Comfort Zone"

One manufacturing plant where we worked stated
that they held the "Gold Medal" standard within
their organisation internationally. Our response was

---

[2] Noel M. Tichy and Stratford Sherman (1994), *Control Your
Destiny or Someone Else Will*, Harper Business.

to demonstrate that the "gold medal" standard within their company was well below true world class manufacturing standards; effectively, they were a big fish in a small pond.

A large charitable organisation had considerable difficulty in contemplating change to the degree required to provide a first class service to clients. Our response was to highlight the vulnerability of the organisation (i.e. that there could be no complacency with regard to their very survival). The potential diminution of their role with clients and the possibility of a great tradition becoming redundant provided the fuel to tackle key changes required by the organisation.

In each of the above, the consulting role is to "hold up a mirror" to an organisation's current practices. Where these are less than complimentary, the dissonance that this causes can provide the energy for moving forward. Without this "fuel" (what we have earlier described as either pain-driven or vision-inspired change strategies) there is no organisation energy and the "body at rest remains at rest". The consulting role is to highlight the current picture in an open, authentic fashion. The managerial role is to decide what to do about this — including "doing nothing" if they do not accept the diagnosis or its implications. Dissonance often provides the lever to engage the management team in a debate about what currently exists and the best way forward.

Can You Over-cook it? How Strong should the Dissonance Be?

The degree of dissonance is a judgement call and partly depends on the quality of the consultant–client relationship (in a sense, it is a measure of how well the "entry" phase has worked). As a rule of thumb, the greater the degree of resistance, the more dissonance will need to be brought to bear. However, using dissonance as a lever to promote debate requires a good degree of personal courage.

One consultant we worked with formally described one of his client organisations as "technical giants and social pygmies". This single phrase (more than the reams of "factual" data presented) caught the management team's attention and provided a pivotal point in a change of direction with regard to how their people were managed.

This is *not* an argument that major organisational change initiatives can turn on a single phrase — however cleverly constructed. It does, however, copper-fasten the view that engaging the senior management team at the front-end is the explanatory factor in successful consulting projects — a point mirrored in many of "best practice" organisation change models. For example, the Kotter model detailed on the next page[3] underscores the point that management commitment is a critical ingredient in successful change. Without this ingredient, change programmes are unlikely to "travel".

---

[3] John A. Kotter (1995), "Leading Change: Why Transformation Efforts Fail", *Harvard Business Review*, April/March.

Eight Steps to Transforming Your Organisation

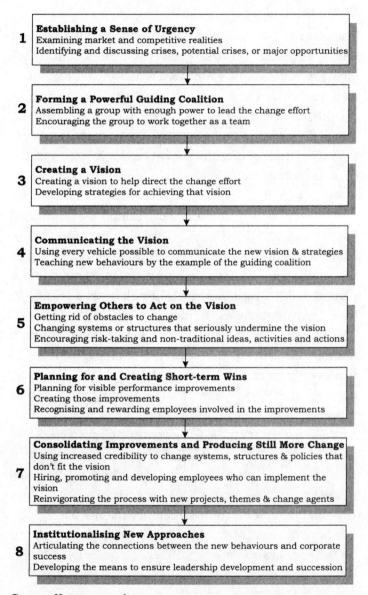

1 **Establishing a Sense of Urgency**
Examining market and competitive realities
Identifying and discussing crises, potential crises, or major opportunities

2 **Forming a Powerful Guiding Coalition**
Assembling a group with enough power to lead the change effort
Encouraging the group to work together as a team

3 **Creating a Vision**
Creating a vision to help direct the change effort
Developing strategies for achieving that vision

4 **Communicating the Vision**
Using every vehicle possible to communicate the new vision & strategies
Teaching new behaviours by the example of the guiding coalition

5 **Empowering Others to Act on the Vision**
Getting rid of obstacles to change
Changing systems or structures that seriously undermine the vision
Encouraging risk-taking and non-traditional ideas, activities and actions

6 **Planning for and Creating Short-term Wins**
Planning for visible performance improvements
Creating those improvements
Recognising and rewarding employees involved in the improvements

7 **Consolidating Improvements and Producing Still More Change**
Using increased credibility to change systems, structures & policies that don't fit the vision
Hiring, promoting and developing employees who can implement the vision
Reinvigorating the process with new projects, themes & change agents

8 **Institutionalising New Approaches**
Articulating the connections between the new behaviours and corporate success
Developing the means to ensure leadership development and succession

Source: Kotter, op. cit.

Toning down the Language at the Client's Request

Sometimes a consultant can make the wrong call and clients have a strongly negative reaction to the language used. Two responses are typical:

a) *Clients feel that the consultant has overstated the case*: Sometimes clients argue that the consultants have been overly negative. As the very nature of organisational diagnosis is to focus on "what's broken", this is a factor that needs to be managed. We completed one memorable diagnostic report for a manufacturing company in the healthcare industry. Some of the managers reacted so negatively to the feedback and the way it was documented that we were asked, literally, to tear up the report. The fear was that copies of the report would be seen by the US parent company.

b) *Consultants make some factual errors (wrong names, titles, information, etc.)*: Our general stance is to modify language at the client's request — up to a point. If the suggested changes "water down" the central findings, the consultant is faced with an ethical dilemma; we would normally resist this. We try to overcome this potential negative by the inclusion of a "standard paragraph" at the front of reports.

> The document is based on a rudimentary understanding of the business and is for discussion purposes only at this point. We have made some working assumptions that may need to be modified later. If there are errors of

fact we can correct these at the discussion stage.

Additional methods to help clients "accept" feedback are the use of comparative data and models. Both of these are explored below.

Use of Comparative Data: Benchmarking "Us" versus "Them"

Comparative data (where this is available) can help to convince a sceptical audience of the need to change or convince them of the "size of the gap". Obviously, care has to be taken to use points of relevant comparison ("apples versus apples"). Nothing focuses the collective managerial mind like discovering that a "sister" plant/competitor has 30 per cent better on-time delivery (or whatever).

Using Models to Help Communicate the Gap in Performance

One senior manager in the banking sector described his job as "Director of Fog Clearance". It was a great role description at a time when his organisation was faced with a number of contradictory choices. In many ways, this title is apt for the role played by consultants; providing clarity is a key element of the data feedback stage.

A useful mechanism to help clients gauge their current status is to use a model of best practice and highlight how well the organisation is performing against this. For example, in response to the question, "How well is our management team performing?", it is possible to contrast current practices against a "best practice" list such as the one below.

World-Class Management Team Criteria[4]	How do we compare?
1. Shared/common purpose/clear strategy	
2. Stretch Targets: Short-term goal of improved performance (with specific metrics assigned)	
3. Clear understanding of short-term roadblocks (12–18 month)	
4. Appropriate leadership (includes boundary management with external groups)	
5. Managerial processes which are effective and economical in time usage	
6. Strong team. Independent, career-oriented managers. Sense of control over own destiny (not "schoolboys")	
7. Robust personal relationships. Conflicts can be openly expressed, dealt with. The openness is often tempered with a sense of fun/humour	
8. Mutual interdependency (notion of internal customer service)	
9. Rewarded for excellence	

Models can also be used to support understanding of complex organisational issues. For example, in relation to helping companies introduce teamworking, it is important to understand the essential dif-

---

[4] The list is an amalgam of ideas from various readings on effective teamwork and also based on our own experience in working with executive teams.

ference between project teams and full-blown team-based organisations. We developed the following model for use with one client organisation to make this distinction clearer.

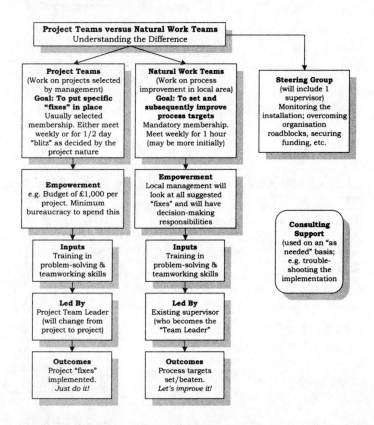

Overall, the use of models can help clients conceptualise issues. Access to models presupposes familiarity with the relevant literature and/or the conceptual ability to develop in-house models. Either way, the endgame is the same — to help clients understand complex organisational issues that may lie outside their sphere of competence. The use of "models" to help companies understand complex issues is illustrated in our next example.

CarCo: Elaborating our Values

In 1998 we became involved with a major Irish company, helping them to elaborate and internally market their values. The issue of "organisation values" is complex; we have seen many examples where companies took an overly simplistic approach to this — elaborating a set of concepts and simply publishing these internally. The benefit is speed. The downside is that nothing happens (other than the creation of internal cynicism if the company does not live up to the stated values).

In order to help this company fully appreciate the complexity surrounding the topic of organisation values and the need to install these properly, we developed the following listing:

Upsides of clearly articulated Organisational Values:

a) Provides clarity of purpose *for the organisation and expectations of behaviour for the members. Where organisational values become shared beliefs (i.e. they are internalised by the members of the organisation), they give a unity of purpose and a common focus of effort direction. Extraordinary attention is paid by managers to whatever is stressed in the corporate value system. Essentially, the corporate values statement answers the question: "How will we do business?"*

b) Lessens need for overt control. *Shared values lessen the need for supervision and provide indirect control. In essence, people supervise themselves and become "their own policeman". In organisations spread across a number of geographical locations, this is a particularly useful benefit in terms of both effectiveness and cost efficiency.*

c) Unleashes energy towards the "cause". *Knowledge workers cannot be controlled and need to work towards a "higher cause". Values provide an identity with an organisation that stands for something noble. People are emotional beings and noble values raise energy levels. People become dedicated to the "cause" (i.e. something more than shareholder value).*

d) Speeds decision-making. *Values are especially useful when they are shared. They provide criteria for decision-making across an organisation (e.g. "how should we respond to this specific customer complaint?")*

e) Everyone can participate. *The simplicity of a values statement makes it usable at all organisational levels. Unlike strategic plans, which can only be accessed by the "corporate few", values have a relevance to everyone in the organisation.*

f) Helps drive/install organisational change. *Articulating company values can provide support for a "new" organisation when new behaviours are required (i.e. it can be a useful mechanism in internal change programmes).*

g) Creates external image. *Clearly articulated values can help to portray the company to the outside world (values are often used in advertising slogans — potential upside for the company in investor relations?).*

h) Provides a benchmark. *Companies tend to evaluate external services/supplies against their own values.*

Downsides of clearly articulated Organisational Values:

a) Potential for cynicism. *It creates cynicism if the management team do not follow through on the stated values. Organisations are much better off to "stay silent" on their values rather than to articulate a set of values that are not practised.*

b) Employees will hold you to account. *It challenges the organisation to live up to the values. For example, what do you do with a manager who achieves good results but does not live by the organisation values?*

c) It's not free! *The installation of the values programme needs time (initially just to understand the concept), emotional energy and continual internal marketing. Values are not "free". To work, they need to become part of the ongoing management agenda.*

Reducing a complex topic to a "manageable" number of issues helps executive teams to focus their key resource — time — on the issues that matter most.

When Models Confuse the Client: Don't be too Clever

If the purpose of using a model is to bring clarity, care must be taken not to overcomplicate it. We "dropped the ball" on this in our next illustration.

ProcessorCo: Design of the Training System

In early 1998, we were involved with a major manufacturing company in the electronics sector. The job was to look at their current management development system, benchmark this against best practice and determine what needed to be done to "close the gap".

After "sweating the details" (by looking at their current practices and all of the relevant literature) we came to the conclusion that management training/development was really composed of two separate streams of activity, operating side-by-side. The first stream was a range of actual development activities (e.g. off-the-job training programmes); the second stream was a range of organisational "supports" (e.g. performance coaching by a person's direct boss).

Having mentally "figured this out" with the support of another consultant, I decided that it should be relatively easy to capture this in a "Management Development Framework" model — (reproduced on the next page).

The result: *A confused client who could not relate to the complexity of the model. He accused us of obfuscation and introducing unnecessary complexity — the exact opposite of the original intention. In developing models, the consultant can become emotionally attached to their own creation/cleverness and lose sight of the primary question: "Will this help the client?"*

The Non-commercial Sector can be a Real Challenge

In my experience, the voluntary/non-commercial sector — where the "coin of the realm" is power and politics, rather than money — represents some of the most "difficult-to-change" organisations. In this sector, particular care needs to be taken about "sensitivities" to the data presented. Issues like the level of participation, exactly who should be involved, etc., are often invested with a deeper meaning and need to become carefully managed, as the next case illustrates.

MANAGEMENT DEVELOPMENT FRAMEWORK

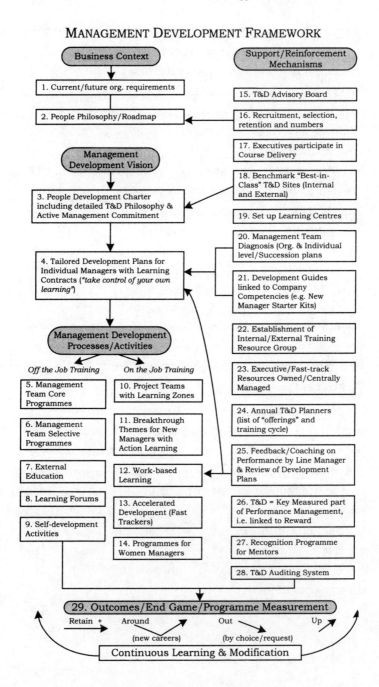

VolunteerOrg: Overhauling the Administration

We were involved in one significant change project with an organisation that historically had little central control and allowed maximum autonomy to its membership. When circumstances changed — with a need for a radical overhaul of the organisation's methods — this proved extremely difficult. In designing this change project, we anticipated this difficulty in three ways.

a) Data collection: *At the data collection stage we involved a huge number of people — much more than was needed, strictly speaking, simply to diagnose the issue. The involvement level was driven by a need to ensure this group would support the eventual outcome.*

b) Feedback of interim results: *At the mid-way point, we "tested" the emerging data through an exhaustive communications roadshow. This allowed the group to challenge some of the emerging issues and, in a subtle way, to begin to factor this into their thinking.*

c) Publication of a working draft: *At the final stage we put together a "working draft" report, distributed it to the membership, and changed several elements of the final presentation.*

It was a long route to get to the destination — but it was ultimately successful in that the organisation did manage to change its modus operandi.

*Organisation change programmes that do not pro-
duce organisation change are not "better" because
they were completed quickly. While this holds for
all types of organisations, in the voluntary/non-
commercial sector, it is particularly relevant.*

The "Whoosh" Factor: Now you Know You're "Getting Hot"

In the children's game "blind man's bluff", the person who is "it" (i.e. has their eyes covered) is guided
to the target with the phrases "you're getting hot" or
"you're getting cold". The same logic may partly apply to handling feedback meetings.

In feeding back information to groups, consultants often encounter a "whoosh factor". Because the
information can be quite painful to the clients, they
often look for some mechanism to "reduce the dissonance". One obvious target is the consultant —
with translation from "I don't like the message" to "I
don't like the messenger". The "whoosh factor" can
be overt (one manager in a large group meeting
which I facilitated remarked: "I've seen smarter consultants than you come and go here"); or covert ("It
is a highly technical industry. You cannot be blamed
for not fully understanding all of the surrounding
issues"). Consultants must steel themselves for
some amount of negative feedback — and see this as
part of the process of moving forward, rather than as
a personal attack.

Between 9 a.m. and 5 p.m., They Don't Hate Me (But They Might Hate My "Role")

I well remember one particular experience — working with a large (80+) group of managers at a meeting. I was about five minutes into an "introduction" when one of the managers put up his hand to catch my attention. I stopped talking and he stood up and made the following statement "I don't mind being here — as long as you don't expect me to play any f***ing schoolboy games". When he finished he sat down. I explained the rationale for the design of the meeting and asked him if he would give me the "benefit of the doubt" for the morning and we would pick up on this conversation again after lunch. He agreed and we were able to move forward (with me somewhat rattled — but thankfully the morning worked well).

During these times, it is difficult not to feel personally "threatened" and anxious. One way to cope with this is to realise that the ire is not directed at me personally (i.e. clients often don't know me well enough not to like me) but at my *role* as a consultant. In this way, it is possible to have a form of "psychological armour plating", 9 a.m. to 5 p.m.

Encountering the "whoosh" factor is positive, in the sense that the resistance is overt and can be openly addressed. It can signal that the consultant is getting close — touching on sensitive organisation issues. With apologies to Kipling, the need to "keep your head when all about you are losing theirs and blaming it on you", to trust yourself when the client doubts you — and make allowance in the billing too!

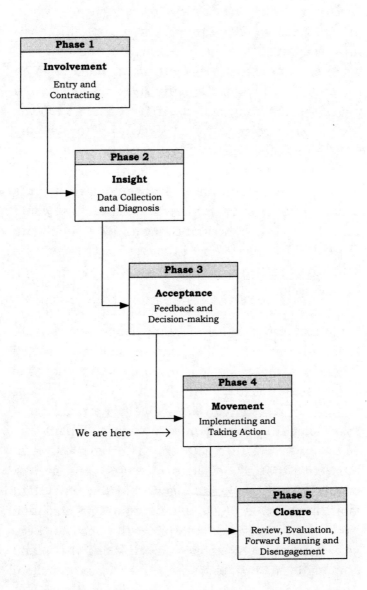

Phase 4

Movement
Implementing and Taking Action

"Everything depends on execution.
Having just a vision is no solution"
— Stephen Sondheim

The purpose of the implementation phase

1. Business is not a university; results pay the bills.

2. Reports, diagnoses, etc. only become *valuable* when they are put into practice.

Moving towards implementation — Phase 4 — involves carrying out the plans developed between the consultant and the management team during the previous phases. In some cases, implementation may lie entirely with the organisation; for other improvement efforts, the consultant can continue to be involved in a range of roles.

Based on my experience to date, this is one of the most difficult stages in the consulting relationship. The dilemma for many organisations is that they often want to "go it alone" at this point — jettisoning the expense of external support. This fits neatly with the process consulting model detailed earlier, where the goal of consultants is to "make themselves redundant" as soon as possible. However, a common dilemma is that managers often get sucked into the vortex of operational problems and "underfund" the change process. Normally organisations cannot overburden a manager who is coping with a huge day-job, expecting them to add a significant additional "change-job" workload. Something has to give.

A Structural Solution to Managing Change Projects

Because of normal business pressures, the "day job" often subsumes the "change job". It is generally not because the management team are "bad managers" (i.e. lack skills). Even where there is a will to implement change, a key missing ingredient is often a defined structure or mechanism to make it happen.

To overcome the gravitational pull of the day job (which soaks the life-blood from managers and ensures that the change job gets inadequate attention), projects need to be "structured" for success, that is:

- Given sufficient managerial time — often by freeing managerial resources from the current "day job".

- If external support is used, given sufficient consultant time and the resources that this implies.

- Producing sufficient senior management attention — often in the form of a steering group or other *defined* support to keep the change project "top of the agenda".

Making it (Relatively) Simple: Keeping the Client "with the Project"

Even well-defined change projects are generally messy affairs and clients are often confused about the questions: "Where are we going?" and "Where are we at now?" Sometimes, it can be helpful if the consultant develops a change "roadmap" and shows the client the route being followed. HR staff at GE have used the following model to explain/guide the transformation process at that company. Similar in-house models have fairly wide application.

CHANGE BEGINS BY ASKING WHO, WHY, WHAT AND HOW

Key Success Factors for Change	Questions to Assess and Accomplish these Key Factors
Leading change *(Who is responsible?)*	Do we have a leader . . . • who owns and champions the change? • who publicly commits to making it happen? • who will garner the resources necessary to sustain it? • who will put in the personal time and attention needed to follow through?

Key Success Factors for Change	Questions to Assess and Accomplish these Key Factors
Creating a shared need *(Why do it?)*	Do employees . . . • see the reason for the change? • understand why it is important? • see how it will help them and the business in the short and long term?
Shaping a vision *(What will it look like when we are done?)*	Do employees . . . • see the outcome of the change in behavioural terms (that is, in terms of what they will do differently as a result of the change)? • get excited about the results of accomplishing the changes? • understand how it will benefit customers and other stakeholders?
Mobilising commitment *(Who else needs to be involved?)*	Do the sponsors of the change . . . • recognise who else needs to be committed to the change to make it happen? • know how to build a coalition of support for the change? • have the ability to enlist support of key individuals in the organisation? • have the ability to build a responsibility matrix to make the change happen?

Key Success Factors for Change	Questions to Assess and Accomplish these Key Factors
Modifying systems and structures (How will it be institutionalised?)	Do the sponsors of the change . . . • understand how to link it to other HR systems such as staffing, training, appraisal, rewards, structure and communication? • recognise the systems implications of the change?
Monitoring progress (How will it be measured?)	Do the sponsors of the change . . . • have a means of measuring its success? • plan to benchmark progress against both the results of the change and the process of implementing it?
Making it last (How will it get started and last?)	Do the sponsors of the change . . . • recognise the first steps in getting started? • have a short-term and long-term plan to keep attention focused on the change? • have a plan to adapt the change over time?

Swim Upwards away from Your E-mail: The Discipline of Project Planning

A key success factor in management projects is to create sufficient headroom — space in which to devote time to nurture the change process. In an increasingly turbulent environment, managers are bombarded with information and "organisational noise". To illustrate: we worked with a general manager in Cork on a small strategic planning project. During his one-day absence, he received 68 e-mail messages, 15 phone calls (all "urgent") and about six personal "interruptions". I asked him if he was having a crazy day. His reply was, "No, it's running about normal".

On a visit to Dublin, Tom Peters referred to this behaviour as the "in-tray" school of management and e-mail is particularly sneaky in this regard. Some systems have a flashing signal on the monitor, informing managers of new incoming mail. It's difficult to resist such temptation. There could be big news breaking. Usually it's small news — and further distraction from a manager's key objectives. Given that this is the "normal" management environment, it makes great sense to put change projects onto a formal project management footing. We can illustrate with two "war stories" — one which worked, one which didn't.

The Headcount Reduction Project

MoneyCo: when it works

We had a contract with one of the large financial service institutions to help them reduce their managerial headcount. In an organisation that had tolerated underperformance for many years, this was big news. The structure was relatively simple. The "Top 10" (worst performers) were identified by the management team. Various options were then worked out for each manager

(early retirement; possible consultancy roles, etc.).
Their line managers then held a series of meetings
with each identified manager and worked through
the steps of the programme — eventually moving
them out of the organisation.

Sitting on top of this structure was a small
team (the MD, the HR manager and myself) and
we "rode shotgun" on the programme implementa-
tion. We met every Monday morning for about an
hour and a half to review progress. During the
week, the HR manager kept track of progress and
had this data for our Monday meeting. The project
was accomplished on time and on budget, and
was deemed extremely successful.

MortgageCo: when it doesn't

In contrast, we worked on a similar job in another
large organisation. The planning was completed in
the same way (individuals selected, options de-
cided, financial planned). All the ingredients for
the cake were on the table — but it was never
baked. Both because of the awkwardness of the
issue[1] and the lack of a formal system of imple-
mentation, the plan was never followed through.

---

[1] In the financial world, long service is typical. Thus, senior
managers may be faced with firing a manager who joined the
company over 25 years ago. They may have "soldiered" together in the local branch for years. Their families probably
know each other well. Into this mix is introduced the notion
that one manager will "fire" the other for poor performance.
In lots of cases it simply does not happen.

Project Management: The "Portacabin Technique"

Changing organisations (installing new systems, running outplacement programmes, etc.) is complex. In this, we can take a lead from building site foremen — what might be labelled the "Portacabin School of Management". The central point in construction project planning is that someone has a blueprint, a plan with a defined timescale and systematically follows through on this. "Did you finish the wiring?"; "I need you to order the plumbing materials"; "Why are we delayed on the window installation?"; etc.). Organisations need "managerial portacabins" (in the form of defined structures) to ensure that change projects get sufficient attention and funding (management time/consulting money).[2] As a generalisation, we see little shortage of strategic *thinking* but a woeful lack of strategic *implementation*, which is the Achilles heel of organisation improvement projects. Our next case illustrates this point.

The Performance Management System in "PharmCo"

We were asked to design and install a Performance Management System for a mid-size manufacturing company in rural Ireland. We knew the

---

[2] Several companies dedicate "change rooms" — physically separate structures — as a method to underpin change management.

company fairly well — having worked with them on a couple of previous projects. The company had expressed a high need for self-sufficiency (to lead projects themselves) and cost-effectiveness (while they did use consultants, the usage was minimal).

We spent the first meetings with the full management team trying to understand their objectives for the new system. Off-line we designed a "strawman" performance management process (how it would work, formats, etc.) and agreed this with the management team in a subsequent meeting. They were happy with the work and stated that they wished to "go it alone" on the implementation; we "slipped away into the night".

About one year later, the company contacted us again on an unrelated project. A number of production issues were causing them concern and we visited the plant to investigate. When we began to "unravel" the presenting issues, it became clear that the redesigned performance management system had never been fully installed. In fact, it had "gone off the rails" within about one month of the initial launch.

Telling a story that we see continually replayed, the management team informed us that the day job had ramped up and swallowed the change job. Because we had not been involved with the company in the installation, we had been unaware of this.

The dilemma here is that once a change programme has been "launched" unsuccessfully, it is more difficult to recover for a second attempt; birth

> *is easier than reincarnation. The relaunch of an
> internal programme has to overcome a hill of scep-
> ticism which usually greets programmes on their
> "second time around".*

Take a lesson from gardening. We planted six euca-
lyptus trees in the back garden of our house. The
ground was prepared well. The trees seemed strong
and healthy, looked well and made good initial progress. All went well until our boxer dog discovered a
new place to "mark out his territory". The trees died.
In organisations, many change programmes similarly begin life positively and look good initially.
However, to be successful, change programmes need
continual reinforcement and to be kept safe from
"organisational dogs".

Keys to Success for Implementation of a Performance Management System

Working more closely with the second implementation, we helped the company in the example above
to develop the following "four-step" plan to install a
working performance management system.

Step #1: System Design

- Implement a single system across all businesses.

- Good format design. "User-friendly" paperwork.

- Format included an explicit behaviour element.

- Measuring individual contribution as part of a project team.

- End of year "ranking and rating" to ensure consistency.

- Need for clear process for managing under-performance.

- Strong link to pay.

Step #2: Internal Marketing

- Strong communication of rationale.

- No "opt out" facility for any manager.

- Sweet stuff: Full "merchandising", e.g. booklets for employees, senior executive; launch video, managerial handbook, etc.

- Sour stuff: In place for two years, then "we will listen" to redesign arguments.

Step #3: Role Modelling

- Systematically practised by senior managers.

- Installation is the key measurement for senior executives.

- Actual time commitment specified:

Training Commitment	8 hours
Development of Annual Plan	6 hours
Assist Individuals with *their* Planning	2 hours
Interim Coaching	4 hours

Annual Review/Salary Adjustment   4 hours

Argument: This is a realistic time investment

Step #4: High Impact Training

There are two elements: mechanical and behavioural.

- Mechanical: "process" made crystal clear.

- Skills training in all segments, e.g. communicating salary decision, constructive confrontation etc.

- Incremental methodology: train close to "usage".

- Mandatory attendance at training.

Internal Marketing of the Need for Change: Seeing is Believing

In the successful management of change, there is often a need to overcome internal scepticism. In many companies the management team have been crying "wolf" for years (everything from new technology to Far Eastern competition). When the real "wolf" arrives, employees can be sceptical. There are a number of ways to overcome this (as one insurance salesman selling death benefits described it: "to let them smell the flowers"). Our next illustration demonstrates this point.

SweetCo: The "imported wolf" is eating our lunch!

We were hired to assist a large food manufacturer in responding to an external competitive threat. A low-cost substitute product was being imported. In 24 months the competitor had increased their market share from 5 per cent to 18 per cent. To counteract this, a range of internal changes needed to be made quickly.

The staff were sceptical. The suggested changes were seen as a management ploy to drive higher levels of productivity — unrelated to any external threat. They had heard it all before — in spades — "from a succession of new managers who have tried to make their careers on our sweat". It needed something different — but what?

We bought large quantities of the competitor product, opened the packaging and literally spilled it onto the floor of a meeting room. We then did the same with the client's product. Over the two mounds of product we printed up a huge sign, which asked:

"Question: *What's the difference between theirs and ours?*
Answer: *80p per kilo."*

To copper-fasten the message, we set up taste tests with the shop stewards and the general workforce, to see if they could taste the difference between the products. They couldn't and were finally convinced of the external threat. The change programme started to roll forward.

None of the examples selected are designed to project the notion that any single idea — no matter how cleverly constructed — will determine the outcome of a change management programme. Change programmes are organisational marathons; a brilliant first mile will not suffice. However, sometimes creativity can help to get the process moving forward.

Keep an Eye on the "Soft Stuff": The Importance of Symbolism

In working through change projects, the importance of symbolism is sometimes underestimated. Managers need to become skilled at "social engineering". We can illustrate this with our next example.

AirCo: Stitching the Pieces Together — The Jigsaw Story

We were involved with one large company that had a problem in getting all of the management team aligned behind a common vision. There were many "potential futures" and some internal debate as to the relative merits of each. We worked with the senior team (50+ managers) for two days, crafting a strategy for going forward.

At the end of the session we unveiled an aerial photograph of their facility. It was about six feet high and ten feet wide and laminated onto quarter-inch blockboard. This photo had then been cut into a jigsaw. In a "commitment ceremony" at the end of the workshop, each manager was invited to take a piece of the jigsaw, symbolising that each person had a part to play in the future of the organisation. Months later, I noticed the jigsaw pieces on permanent display in individual managers' offices, acting both as a memento and as a reminder of their role on the management team.

Bottom line: New systems in organisations need support to "bed in". It is analogous to planting a tree in your garden. The soil needs to be prepared and the new tree needs a stake for the first two years of its life. Within organisations, change programmes wither without this initial level of commitment and support.

Leadership Energises Change Projects

"Today's employee is over-managed and under led"
— Dr. Warren Bennis

We were involved in a particularly interesting customer service project with one of the main retail banking organisations in Ireland. A "capture" of the main case points is outlined below.

CardCo: Full Diagnosis versus Speed —
Managing the Trade Off

We met the newly appointed Managing Director of a bank subsidiary company operating in Dublin. There were over 120 people employed in the business, which operated from a city centre office. Company performance has been somewhat lacklustre (the business lost several million pounds in the previous year on a turnover of over £400 million).[3] The MD was a young recent hire, ex-Arthur Andersen, being "blooded" on this job to see if he could turn the organisation around. His job was to turn around the business and to re-energise the people. He had an 18-month timeframe to get the company "into the black".

An internal strategy team identified customer service as being a critical success factor for the business. The MD looked for external consultants to help him work on this specialist area and we became involved at that stage.

With no experience of this particular company, we needed to get a better definition of exactly what customer service improvements should be made, what they would cost and how they might impact the business. It also had to be done quickly, as the business was "haemorrhaging money".

---

[3] Actual numbers have been changed to protect confidentiality.

*I have a vivid memory of that first meeting —
descending the stairs, "buzzing" with various possible approaches to the problem. After a couple of
days we met again with the MD. We told him we
did not have enough data to go forward and laid
out a range of information requirements. For
example, the company did not fully understand
their customer base. Key questions needed to be
addressed around how customers were seg-
mented: why people used the basic product was
unclear; what products were profitable, what
products were loss-making, etc. I presented the
scenario of "too little information" to the MD and a
plan to collect this. Once we had this baseline
data, we could go forward.*

*He listened patiently, waiting for me to finish
my pitch. He then said: "This business is losing its
shirt. The questions you are raising sound like
good stuff but while you are completing your diagnosis, I will be losing £10,000 each working
day. I need something to kick in much faster." We
were following the Einstein School ("A problem
well-framed is a problem half-solved"). He has a
business to run. Suitably chastened, we decided
to use a talking wall[4] exercise.*

The "talking wall" technique

---

[4] Officially labelled metaplanning. "Talking wall" is a more apt
term.

Directly after the second meeting, we developed a list of the six most important questions which we wanted the staff to answer. These were:

1. Maintaining our existing customers: *How can we retain all of our existing customers?*

2. Competition: *Do our competitors offer any element of superior service?*

3. External Customer Service: *In the next 12 months, to improve our current level of external customer service (retailers and cardholders), we should . . . ?*

4. Internal customer service: *In the next 12 months, to improve our current level of internal customer service (Internal departments/ branches, etc.) we should . . . ?*

5. Past 12 months: *Were there some things that we tried to change but were not successful? What could we do to correct these?*

6. Overcoming roadblocks: *Are there any factors (organisational, managerial, technological, etc.) which block or limit our efforts to deliver world-class customer service?*

We then took over an internal meeting room, papering the walls with flip chart paper. On this paper we sprayed 3M "Mount Spray" — a sticky substance used by graphic designers. Once this was completed, it was possible to stick "cards" onto the flip chart sheets and later remove these — similar to the "post-it notes" concept, except on a larger scale. We divided the 120 staff into groups of six (i.e. 20 people in each group). Over a day and a half, we ran six meetings, each lasting an hour and a half. The format for each meeting was as follows:

1. The MD introduced the meeting and explained our involvement. Essentially, he told the staff that the business was "in a hole" and asked for their help in resolving this.

2. We then asked each staff member to individually "brainstorm" solutions to the six key questions posed above. What happened next was one of the most extraordinary consulting experiences detailed in the book. The 120 staff generated an incredible 4,230 "ideas for improvement" — an extraordinary 35 ideas per person on average. Given the right conditions, staff are "oil gushers" of creativity and this exercise demonstrated this.

The secret to success: follow-through

In the property business they say that the three secrets of success are location, location and location. In management, the three secrets of success may well be implementation, implementation and implementation.

The individual ideas were pulled together. As a first step, "duplicate" ideas were merged, which left over 900 individual ideas. These were then ranked into A = excellent, B = good, C = possible

*and D = no categories. The criteria for an "A" idea
was as follows:*

1. *It had to have a visible, positive impact on customer service.*

2. *It had to be relatively easy to implement.*

3. *It had to be low cost to implement.*

*The "A" ideas represented about 10 per cent of the
pool. These were put onto project management
software and communicated to staff. Staff were
given an opportunity to push "B" ideas onto the
"A" list. Once the "A" list was finalised, the closure of "A" items was clinically well managed.
This is execution "par excellence" and a wonderful
demonstration of the power of leadership to drive
both a business and a staff agenda side by side.*

Epilogue: *Within 12 months, the business was
"in the black" and has been phenomenally successful since that time.*

Learning from the Past: What has Already Been Tried?

"Those who forget the past are condemned to repeat it"
— *Santayana*

There is a well-worn axiom in the consultancy business: "If you wish to understand an organisation, try
to change it." By attempting to change an organisation, it is possible for a consultant to "uncover" elements of the culture that are covert — kept below

the waterline. Often, useful insights can be gleamed by looking at previous change efforts. Our next example takes us back into the food industry.

"FoodCo: Do the Supervisors need more Training?

We were asked to design a training programme for a group of middle-level managers in the food sector. Several problems with this group's performance were outlined in detail in a briefing note sent to us by the Personnel Director; we were to design a training programme to "close the gaps" and overcome the performance problems identified.

Ergo

The problem identified: Lack of skills.
The problem resolved: Skills training.
During our initial meeting with the group of trainees, we discovered that:

1. *Sixty per cent of them had been through a formal external supervisory development programme in the past three years.*

2. *A previous management development programme had been run internally and specifically addressed several of the topics which we were asked to include in our programme.*

Not surprisingly, we did not feel that the problems presented represented a "training issue" or would be open to being resolved through addition inputs.

We engaged the management team in a wider route forward — Organisation Development. The logic here is not difficult to understand. If two previous attempts to resolve an issue have not proven successful, there is a good likelihood that the "search for oil" has been happening in the wrong place.

The three reasons why people don't perform

We began to work with this company, helping them to "segment" performance problems into one of three categories:

1. *People don't perform because they don't know (lack of clarity/educational issue).*
2. *People don't perform because they don't know how (lack of skills).*
3. *People don't perform because they don't want to (lack of motivation).*

Armed with this categorisation of reasons for non-performance, we were able to help the organisation diagnose the root cause and (eventually) to move forward on this. We did this by working directly with the supervisory group to agree a new definition of their role. The process followed is detailed below:

Step 1 *(working in small teams of supervisors; all supervisors in the room)*

1. *The team appointed a facilitator.*

2. *Each person working individually developed a listing of issues addressing the following question:* "In terms of managing in this industry, what is expected from each supervisor in our company?"

3. *The listing was kept to the seven or eight "big issues" without getting into too much detail at this point.*

4. *Once completed, the group shared/recorded the responses on the flip charts provided.*

Step 2 *(plenary session)*

1. *Each group made a presentation to the entire team on the work they had completed in the previous exercise.*

2. *Once this had taken place, the session was opened to the entire team, where the questions* "Have we missed anything/Can we really deliver on this?" *were used to challenge each presentation.*

3. *The agreed listing of headings formed the basis for the next exercise.*

Supervisors at the Company Redefined their Role

Following discussion and synthesisation of the individual points, the supervisors at the company defined their role under nine key headings as follows:

1. *Provide a safe working environment*

2. *Control the process*

3. *Deliver high quality products and services*

4. *Maximise hygiene standards throughout the plant*

5. *Maintain plant equipment in optimum condition*

6. *Keep the lid on expenditure/cost control*

7. *Proactively manage industrial relations*

8. *Provide excellent customer service*

9. *Maximise the performance potential of our people.*

Step 3 *(return to small teams)*
The purpose of this session was to understand the exact detailed requirements of the role of supervisors at the company.

Breakout Team Instructions

1. *Each team member wrote down individually the three or four most important behaviours under each of the nine agreed headings. The instruction was to make these as specific as possible.*

2. *The team shared and recorded all the listings on the flip charts provided.*

3. *The top six most important behaviours under each area were chosen by grouping and synthesising the individual inputs.*

4. *For example, under the heading of "maximise the performance potential of your people", team members might have listed:*

   "Each morning my first job is to walk around the plant and ensure that everyone is at their place of work and 'ready to go' by 8 a.m."

5. *Once completed, team members had to ask themselves the following questions:*

   - *Will these actions really support the development of our company?*

   - *Have I been overly optimistic? Are they achievable?*

   - *Have I been overly pessimistic? Are they too easy to achieve?*

   - *How personally committed do I feel to this listing?*

   - *What will happen these actions now?*

6. *Discussion on next steps forward.*

The teams "brought back" their individual lists of behaviours and these were "rolled up" into a central document.[5] A full outline of the "finished product" is detailed in the Appendix to this chapter.

---

[5] Having done a good job up to this point, we made a tactical error here. In the "roll-up" of the inputs, the language used in the final document became "ours", not "theirs". Ownership of the "writing-up" stage is always a judgement call. On this

AccountingCo: Rolling Back the Future

*We were involved with one financial department
— helping them to develop a vision of the future.
In a single session they constructed the following:*

AccountingCo: Finance Vision

Our vision is to be the best Finance Function
within AccountingCo. We will achieve this
when we have:

a) Quality results produced on time

b) With minimum effort

c) A sound control environment

d) Proactive MIS

e) Supporting our customers' day-to-day
    needs

f) Anticipating issues and opportunities and
    developing commercial solutions for the
    business

g) People: happy, motivated staff.

---

*Once the vision was developed, they began the
detailed planning to turn the aspirations set into
reality.*

---

occasion we called it wrong and the commitment to the final
document was diluted.

Overall, the implementation phase is possibly the most problematical in the consulting cycle. While there is no one best way, successful projects which we've been involved in have all been actively followed through by an active individual manager or management team. On the basis that "results pay the bills" the consulting input only really starts to pay for itself when the implementation phase is successful.

Appendix: Draft Document — Job Description for the Supervisory Group

Q: What is our competitor's fervent wish?
A: That the Company will not change!
It is a wish that will not be granted.

Background
Premises "A" is tasked with producing high quality food at the lowest possible cost. Changes in the external market — with increased competition — have put pressure on the plant to outperform the historical best standards that have been achieved. We are entering a new game.

In order to outperform our previous "best", every single element of the plant's operations has to come under scrutiny — underscored by every member of the management team adopting a philosophy of continuous improvement.

Supervisors Redefine their Role

The Supervisors have now redefined their role under nine key headings:

- *Provide a Safe Working Environment*

- *Control the Process*

- *Deliver High Quality Products and Services*

- *Maximise Hygiene Standards throughout the Plant*

- *Maintain Plant Equipment in Optimum Condition*

- *Keep the Lid on Expenditure/Cost Control*

- *Proactively Manage Industrial Relations*

- *Provide Excellent Customer Service*

- *Maximise the Performance Potential of our People.*

This document captures the essence of the new supervisory role. The attempt here is to detail the complete job descriptions for all categories of supervisors. Not all of the elements detailed apply to every supervisory position at the plant.

---

1. Provide a Safe Working Environment

- *Ensure all safety procedures are understood and adhered to*

- *Continually assess jobs for hazards and re-engineer these*

- *Supply safety equipment and ensure this is worn*
- *Ensure that housekeeping standards contribute to a safe, clean working environment*
- *Continually improve our current safety standards by personally becoming a "safety champion" within your own area of responsibility.*

2. Control the Process

- *Ensure availability of process materials, and optimise their usage*

- *Continually monitor the process — keep it within control specs*

- *Ensure all stations operate correctly — make throughput level adjustments as needed*

- *Analyse and solve problems to reduce cost/ enhance product quality*

- *Ensure all quality and process procedures are adhered to*

- *Maximise reliability/availability of equipment.*

3. Deliver High Quality Products and Services

- *Ensure that all equipment is adjusted/set correctly*

- *Continually carry out inspections (both proactive/reactive)*

- *Improve hygiene/housekeeping in all areas*

- *Conduct tests on an accurate and timely basis*

- *Evaluate process materials from vendors.*

4. Maximise Hygiene Standards throughout the Plant

- *Maintain ISO specifications — as an absolute minimum*

- *Improve on ISO specifications/hygiene standards*

- *Ensure personal hygiene control of all plant operatives*

- *Monitor hygiene control of all garments worn in the plant*

- *Control leaks/overflow*

- *Provide equipment for cleaning*

- *Ensure regular/continuous cleaning is carried out.*

5. Maintain Plant Equipment in Optimum Condition

- *Ensure equipment is "safe" to use*

- *Provide training to operators in equipment use and check operation methods*

- *Ensure correct operation of equipment*

- *Ensure equipment is available for use through regular maintenance*

- *Log history of maintenance on individual equipment*

- *Ensure availability of spares*

- *Highlight process difficulties; put forward solutions to "fix"*

- *Commission new equipment as per the manual specifications.*

6. Keep the Lid on Expenditure/Cost Control

- *Control usage of process materials*

- *Stay within defined budgets*

- *Control hours (overtime and additional helpers)*

- *Identify areas that require extra maintenance*

- *Control usage of steam economy*

- *Control usage of spare parts*

- *Purchase of goods at the lowest price.
  Re-negotiate prices downwards where possible*

7. Proactively Manage Industrial Relations

- *Ensure people are at their stations on time/
  remain until relieved*

- *Maintain/control time-keeping in the off season*

- *Motivate the people within your work group by
  keeping your people up to date on business
  performance*

- *Handle any disciplinary issues/complaints that
  arise at shop floor level and take ownership of
  the resolution of these.*

8. Provide Excellent Customer Service

- *Provide excellent service to customers who come
  to the site*

- *Ensure loads are safe and meet load
  specifications*

- *Support dispatch*
  - ◊ *Availability of all product*
  - ◊ *Reliability of the equipment used*

- *Report complaints to relevant people. Follow up to ensure that the appropriate actions have been taken.*

9. Maximise the Performance Potential of our People

- *Train new operators and communicate the importance of high quality/low cost sugar*

- *Share your knowledge and experience with operators — and listen and learn from our experienced operators about how we can improve the process*

- *Identify the personal development needs of your people and put a put a plan in place to "close the gaps".*

- *Evaluate people's performance with regard to quantity and quality — give timely and authentic feedback*

- *Provide resources, coaching and ongoing support to help people perform*

- *Confront under-performance on a consistent basis — there are no spectators on the pitch*

- *Acknowledge work well done.*

"Catch your people doing something right"

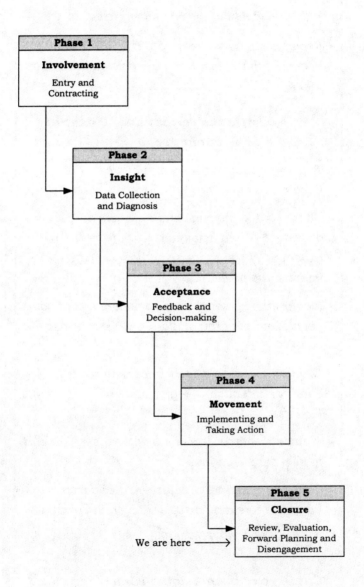

Phase 5

Closure
Review, Evaluation, Forward Planning and Disengagement

The purpose of the closure phase

1. To evaluate the success of the intervention

2. To allow both the client and the consultant to learn from the project

3. To build rapport in order to work together again in the future

---

Consultants Typically have a Defined "Shelf Life"

"Departure" from an organisation can be seen as a positive event, a recognition that the organisation has reached a point of self-sufficiency, where the value the consultant has added has been incorporated into everyday management practice.

There are many options for ending the consulting relationship; termination should be considered a legitimate and important part of the overall consulting cycle. If done well, it can provide an important learning experience for the client and the consultant. It can also keep the relationship positive for future work with the organisation, such as a decision to extend the process to a larger segment of the organisation or to move onto a different project. However, it is our experience that, generally speaking, consultants have a defined "shelf life" within organisations.[1]

The "evaluation phase" focuses on two issues: (i) an evaluation of the "main event"; and (ii) a review of the overall client/consultant relationship.

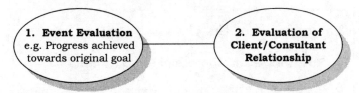

Where a client is reluctant to move away from a consulting link, some consultants deliberately exit the relationship — as our next illustration demonstrates.

Event Evaluation

One way to conduct an "event evaluation" is to assess what happened at each phase of the consulting cycle. The key questions are listed in the figure below.

---

[1] Interestingly, this can be contrasted with internal managers who are seen to "improve"/"mature" over time like good wine.

Phase 1: Involvement
• How well did we complete the contracting stage?
• Were the objectives set explicit/measurable?
• Were the conditions required by both parties met?
• What would we do differently next time?

Phase 2: Insight
• How well did the data collection go?
• What option did we choose?
• Would we do the same next time?
• How would we evaluate the "depth" of insight gained?

Phase 3: Acceptance
• How was the diagnosis received?
• Was this phase managed well?
• What resistance did we meet and how well did we overcome this?
• Next time we will . . . ?

Phase 4: Movement
• What has the "before" versus "after" picture been like?
• What's changed? By how much?
• What is the cost:benefit analysis?
• What remains to be done?

PolicyCo: The Slow, Steady Slide into Dependence

One consultant that we have worked with a number of times secured a particularly good contract. The job entailed him working with a financial services company for two years, guiding an internal change programme. The issues were complex, with a huge investment in technology. Recognising the point that "If you have Formula 1 race cars, you also need skilled drivers", the company decided to invest significant time and energy in developing the "softer" side of the organisation. The particular consultant's role was to facilitate this, guiding the organisation forward.

However, over time he began to notice a subtle change in his role. Officially he was the "facilitator" for the change management project. Unofficially, he became the line manager with responsibility for making it happen. Before decisions were taken, managers would call to "run something by him". Internal managers would ask: "Has Tom OK'd that?" When he tried to renegotiate his role internally to the agreed facilitator role, he was covertly resisted. The organisation came to have a fixed view of how he operated, essentially in the line management role described above. He eventually decided to "leave" the company as he felt he could no longer add value in the original role. The organisation respected that decision and they have maintained a good relationship since (from time-to-time he works on other projects with the company).

Slipping Into the Night: The Silent Consulting Goodbye

Sometimes consultant–client relationships do not have a formal ending, but simply "fizzle out". The consultant may be busy working with other clients and does not have an immediate need for more

business. The client may not have a need for consulting services or may have some issues with the
consultant that are socially awkward to discuss.
These factors can lead to a collusion between consultants and clients to simply "walk away" — a
silent good-bye — without an official funeral. Generally this is negative:

a) *The client*, if they have concerns, should be able to
   table these (albeit some will feel that they do not
   want to invest any more time in the relationship).

b) *The consultant* can lose immense value in getting
   authentic feedback from clients helping them to
   "notch up their game".

Walking away also overlooks the possibility of "service recovery" — the idea that small service mishaps
can often be rescued and this can build even
stronger client loyalty. Sometimes the relationship
fizzles out without any particular reason (a consulting version of "She never phoned, she never wrote").
Our final example offers one possible way to approach this.

HappyCo: They Never Phoned, They Never Wrote . . .

*We sent the following letter (specifics have been
changed) to a client to help us understand why
the relationship had not progressed.*

Mr Joe Dillon
HappyCo
Wexford Road
Co. Dublin

6th January 1998

Dear Joe

You will probably find this note a little "strange", but here goes. Over the Christmas break I have been trying to take stock of 1997 — what worked, what didn't, etc.

Under the "what did not work" category is my relationship with HappyCo. While we seemed to get off to a reasonably good start, by the end of 1997 our relationship had essentially fizzled out.

While there could be any number of reasons for this (poor service, "chemistry", price, etc.), it would be really helpful for me to understand exactly what happened.

When I was the Personnel Manager in Sterling Winthorp, Dungarvan, I well remember a management consultant who pursued work with us non-stop for about three years. I have no wish to become a similar pest to a client company. However, I am well aware of the potential opportunity with HappyCo. and do not want to simply walk away from this.

We should have an authentic discussion to pursue this topic. Give me a buzz when you have some free time and we can review.

Yours sincerely,

Paul Mooney Ph.D.

The letter worked (in the sense that we did have the discussion) and we were able to move onto the next project.

Review and Evaluation Tends to be Underdone

Of the five consulting phases, this chapter is the shortest. It may, in part, reflect our own company style, which is to work with clients on different projects over fairly long periods. Mostly, however, it highlights the general difficulty of conducting reviews when both the client and the consultant have "moved their cross-hairs" onto different projects. Of the five phases detailed, it is the one which we have managed least well — and I suspect this is a representative point for the vast majority of consultants whom I've talked to or worked directly with.

Did you Enjoy the Journey?

I hope that you enjoyed reading this book and managed to glean a couple of ideas (even a couple of "How not to's . . . ") for your organisation. Putting the stories together has helped me to better understand what we do and what we might do better in the future.

Paul Mooney PhD
January 1999

PMA Consulting
205 Mount Prospect Avenue
Clontarf
Dublin 3
Phone Number: 353 1 8330897
Fax Number: 353 1 8335079
E-mail Address: pmaconsult@tinet.ie

Index

Also Available from Oak Tree Press

Developing the High Performance Organisation

Best Practice for Managers

Paul Mooney

ISBN 1 86076 019 8   Price: £19.95   Hardback
ISBN 1 86076 088 0   Price: £16.95   Paperback

Now in paperback, this guide is designed to help practising managers deal with information overload. There are endless books and articles available on various aspects of organisation development, but very few attempt to distil the best thinking world-wide into one practical volume.

This guide will help any manager understand the strategic importance of an organisation's Mission, Vision and Values; the critical need for superior Customer Service; the 20 key principles of Organisation Design; the importance of Performance Planning, Coaching and review; the identification of essential Training Needs and the effective use of Employee Empowerment through Project Teams.

With useful case studies, exercises and practical checklists, *Developing the High Performance Organisation* will show any practising manager how to develop and maintain a World Class organisation that can outperform the competition.

Also Available from Oak Tree Press

Agents of Change

The Manager's Guide to Planning and Leading Change Projects

Hilary Maher and Pauline Hall

ISBN 1 86076 090 2   Price: £16.95   Paperback

Today's volatile work environment means that only the capacity to change can assure the survival of organisations. Whether introducing customer-care initiatives, responding to globalisation, or demands for increased financial accountability, today's managers must cope with the stress and difficulty that introducing change can mean for themselves and their colleagues.

This guide is designed to help practising managers plan for, and manage, change. It provides the essential theories and techniques required to lead the change process, as well as a host of practical ways to use this knowledge in planning and managing change.

Agents of Change is set in a real-life context, with examples of both good and bad practice drawn from current management practice.

The book presents managers with an approach that helps them to minimise the uncertainty and unpredictability of change.

Also Available from Oak Tree Press

Creating and Developing a Consultancy Practice

Martin Wilson

ISBN 1 86076 044 9   Price: £19.95   Paperback

Aimed at anyone planning to move into a consultancy career, and especially those starting their own small practice, *Creating and Developing a Consultancy Practice* is applicable to all consultants providing advisory services to businesses. It is divided into three broad sections as follows:

Part 1: Is Consultancy for You?
This covers what being a consultant is about; the lifestyle and demands; the ups and downs of a consultancy career; the personal issues around aptitude, skills and commitment; etc.

Part 2: Nature of Consultancy
This section explains what consultants do and in broad terms how they go about practising consultancy.

Part 3: The Business of Consultancy
This part covers the marketing work around identifying clients and designing services to meet clients' needs as well as the day-to-day issues around running a practice, such as fees, estimates, sales cycles, what to do when business is slow, etc.

From the author's first-hand experience, *Creating and Developing a Consultancy Practice* is the essential guide to all aspects of setting up in practice and, once there, making that practice a success.